TALL TALES FROM THE HIGH PLAINS & BEYOND
Book Two

I0156984

The

LAW KEEPERS

TOM RIZZO
Author, *Last Stand At Bitter Creek*

TALL TALES FROM THE HIGH PLAINS & BEYOND
Book Two: The Law Keepers

Copyright 2015 © by Tom Rizzo

ISBN-13: 978-0-9847977-5-2
ISBN-10: 0984797750

Cover Design & Interior Layout:
Studio 6 Sense, LLC • www.studio6sense.com

CONTENTS

INTRODUCTION

TALL TALES FROM THE HIGH PLAINS & BEYOND

Book One: The Unexplained and Other Stories

Book Two: The Law Keepers

Book Three: The LawBreakers

When I was growing up, too many years ago, most of the public had a romanticized view of the *Old West* or *Wild West*, as it was known. Western films and novels presented the American West as a place of gambling, gunfights, and Indian raids. Skillful writers and directors developed a formula of storytelling that resulted in perception overriding reality.

Most people who settled in the West didn't wake up in the morning and strap on a gun. Nor did they get involved in shootouts. There's no denying the West presented a rugged and untamed challenge. The characters, conflicts, and creations involved in the actual expansion and development of this new frontier represented fascinating raw material that played such an influential role in American history.

The three books that make up the series *Tall Tales from the High Plains & Beyond* offer short and entertaining stories aimed at giving you an eagle's nest view of the frontier and people who lived and died there. These men and women rival any character you'd meet in the pages of fiction.

- *Book One: The Unexplained and Other Stories* includes tales that border on the bizarre—ghosts, buried treasure, lost gold, a headless horseman, double- and triple-crosses, ambushes, mysterious disappearances, and stories of uncommon courage.

- *Book Two: The Law Keepers* features those who wore the badges of lawmen. Stories of courage, shootouts, showdowns, redemption, retribution, and sweet revenge. Lawmen who sometimes acted outside the law to achieve the desired results.

- *Book Three: The LawBreakers* who roamed the frontier as stone-cold killers, cattle and horse rustlers, bank, stagecoach, and train robbers. Some even tried stepping away from lives of crime and becoming lawmen. Most of those who did, however, discovered it put them in a better position as lawbreakers.

When I went to school, history was little more than memorizing names and facts and figures—an exercise in boredom. History isn't boring—particularly history of the American frontier. It falls to writers and teachers to bring these historical adventures to life, which is what I've tried to do with this series.

Enjoy!

ONE

TIN STAR:
MEN BEHIND THE BADGE

THE SHERIFF SAT AT HIS DESK FIDDLING WITH A TIN CAN, CUTTING, AND BENDING THE METAL TO CREATE A TEMPORARY BADGE THAT WOULD IDENTIFY HIM AS THE LAW.

Since the county never needed a sheriff before, it had no badge to provide the man citizens just elected. The new lawman began having second thoughts about the extent of his new duties and responsibilities. Enforcing the law was only part of the job. He also served as jailer and tax collector, and served warrants, subpoenas, and jury summons.

For the most part, the small and isolated early settlements across the frontier did a good job of self-policing. The majority of those looking to establish a new life and career in the West were honest and law-abiding. Most were friendly, hard working, and trusting—willing to give someone the benefit of the doubt. Growth brought new challenges, including maintaining a peaceful community. Frontier families rarely secured their homes or businesses with locks. Businesses often granted credit without seeking collateral. Western communities took their time establishing a law enforcement arm, but with good reason.

Many settlers who founded the towns were immigrants who previously encountered police abuse and harassment. They harbored a natural distrust for the law. These citizens became the enforcers and often formed vigilante committees. The need emerged for a formal entity to deal with issues of crime at the local level.

The men who wore the badges had to be diligent when it came to enforcing the law. They lacked reliable communication about crimes and criminals. The telegraph helped, but not every community had such service. The U. S. mail provided lawmen with descriptions of criminals, their names, and last known locations. Word-of-mouth helped, as did crude likenesses on wanted posters—also called *dodgers*. But, information traveled at a snail's pace and often was unreliable and outdated by the time it got delivered. The most effective kind of sheriff took a proactive role in the enforcement of frontier justice. A good lawman monitored the arrival of strangers in their towns. He kept tabs on who they were, where they were staying, and why they were visiting.

Sometimes, of course, the town's sheriffs just happened to be criminals themselves. A few changed, went straight, and did their best to uphold the law, and were good at their jobs. Others used their position for financial and political gain and influence. It's no wonder some lawmen crossed to the dark side. The post of sheriff, high in responsibility and visibility, generally didn't pay well.

As a general rule, some counties provided an annual salary of around $200, plus a percentage of any fees the lawmen collected. The fee system differed from territory-to-territory, but, generally reflected this schedule:

- Serving a warrant: $1
- Summoning a juror: $.50
- Summoning the grand jury: $5
- Summoning witnesses: $.50
- Attending court: $1.50
- Calling each witness in court: $.05
- Committing prisoners to jail: $1
- Daily support of prisoners: $.25
- Executing a death warrant: $15
- Travel allowance: $.05 a mile
- Reasonable expenses for other services not specified.

Sheriffs also functioned as the ex-officio tax assessor and collector. The many duties, low pay, and the risks involved often prompted good men to turn bad for the opportunity of more lucrative paydays. The types of crimes lawmen dealt with were too widespread for just one person. The situation provided the perfect opportunity for the advent of bounty hunters. These individuals were in the hunt for the pay-off of reward money. Enterprising individuals created profit-minded private companies to help fill the gap, too. The most well known was Pinkerton National Detective Agency.

Little glamor was associated with role of sheriff. In reality, they spent much of their time serving subpoenas and issuing summons. Lawmen were also responsible for seizing property as directed by civil rulings. They often had to issue summons for a coroner's jury. In some instances, they faced life-and-death situations. Much of their daily work was mundane. As lawmen became more visible, daily life for the town's citizens improved for the better. Citizens began to recognize the need for a legitimate, organized enforcement process, leading to a more peaceful way of life.

TWO

THE
HONORABLE DALTON

WHEN THE TRAIN PULLED INTO THE STATION ON A SUNDAY IN EARLY DECEMBER 1888, IT CARRIED ONE OF THE DALTON BROTHERS. BUT HE WASN'T ABOARD TO ROB IT.

Frank Dalton made the journey from Fort Smith, Arkansas, to Coffeyville, Kansas, in a coffin, the victim of an outlaw's bullet. The 28-year old served as a Deputy US Marshal under Judge Isaac Parker in Indian Territory. His younger brothers—Bob, Emmett, and Grat—became lawman for a while. But all that changed in 1890 when they took off their badges to make their own place in American frontier history as members of the infamous Dalton Gang.

Frank Dalton ranked as the antitheses of his brothers, earning a reputation as a man of unsurpassed courage. Over a three-year period, Marshal Dalton was involved in several shootouts while making high-profile arrests. On November 27,1888, Dalton and Deputy JR Cole tracked horse thief Dave Smith to his camp near the Arkansas River. When the two men approached, Smith fired a rifle from inside a tent, dropping Dalton to the ground with a chest wound. Cole fired back and killed Smith but got wounded in the exchange. Thinking Dalton had been killed, Cole managed to escape.

Dalton, still alive, engaged in a brief gun battle, wounding one of the outlaws. But gang member Will Towerly got the drop on the bleeding lawman, leveled his rifle, and pumped two bullets into Dalton's head. According to a newspaper report, Dalton had begged Towerly not to kill him because he was already near death. An obituary in the Fort Smith Elevator, Dec. 2, 1887, read:

"Frank Dalton was a fearless and efficient officer and an honest up right man, highly esteemed by all who knew him for his many good qualities of head and heart. He was twenty-eight years of age, unmarried and his home being with his mother at Chelsea, Cherokee Nation..."

About a month after Dalton's death, Deputy William Moody and Deputy US Marshal Ed Stokely caught up with Towerly and killed him in a gunfight.

Dalton was buried in Elmwood Cemetery in Coffeyville. Four years later, brothers Bob and Grat would join their elder brother in the same cemetery after being gunned down during a bank robbery attempt in Coffeyville, where the family once lived.

THREE

ONE SHOOTING
TOO MANY

A TROUBLEMAKER BY THE NAME OF SAMUEL STRAWHIM AND A FEW FELLOW TEAMSTERS STORMED THROUGH THE DOORS OF A HAYS CITY, KANSAS, SALOON LATE ONE NIGHT INTENT ON CONTINUING THEIR HELL-RAISING WAYS, BUT THINGS TURNED VIOLENT.

Hays City had the reputation of a wide-open freight and cattle center that attracted gunman of all types, along with buffalo hunters, drifters, and soldiers. Strawhim and his group crowded the bar at John Bitters' Beer Saloon just after midnight on September 27, 1869, and began drinking heavily. After one-drink-too-many, the teamsters' behavior turned ugly. They began wrecking the place—overturning tables, smashing chairs, and engaged in an all-out brawl. Someone summoned help. About 1 a.m., Ellis County Sheriff Bill Hickok and Deputy Peter Lanihan walked into the place to restore law and order.

Hickok ordered Strawhim and his men to stop their conduct and turn over his weapons. But Strawhim wasn't about to comply. He laughed and pulled his guns to challenge the sheriff. Hickok wasted no time, and drew his 1851 Navy Colts. The Hays City *Times and Conservative* reported that Strawhim was "shot and instantly killed by 'Wild Bill' (J.B. Hickok) Sheriff...." Strawhim lay on the floor with a bullet in the head. According to the Hays *Daily News*, Strawhim had served as the community's city-county jailer. An inquest ruled the shooting justifiable homicide.

Wild Bill, at first, was thought to represent the ideal solution to help quell the out-of-control criminal behavior in Hays City, but residents had second thoughts about his aggressive law enforcement methods. In the first five weeks of the job, he had killed two men. In November, he lost the election to his deputy by twenty-five votes. His first job as a law officer lasted only three months.

FOUR

THE SWEETWATER
SHOOTOUT

THE SOLIDER PLAYING CARDS AT LADY GAY SALOON IN Sweetwater, Texas, rose from his chair in disgust, threw his hand down, and stormed out the door. Another player, Bat Masterson, watched him leave. The two would meet again, shortly after midnight.

Corporal Melvin A. King of the 4th Cavalry at a nearby Army post struggled with the cards before leaving the game. The more he lost, the more he drank. During his military career, King developed a serious drinking problem that led to a history of bad behavior. When sober, he often won praises as a good soldier and an accomplished wrangler. Once the game ended on the night of January 24, 1876, Bat Masterson left the table and joined in conversation with black-haired and blue-eyed Mollie Brennan, a well-known soiled dove.

At this point, the specifics of what happened vary from story-teller-to-storyteller. Sweetwater didn't have a newspaper. No official accounts of the tragic incident exist. One version suggests King was angry over the cards Masterson dealt him. Another account tells about Corporal King being sweet on Mollie. Whether she knew how he felt isn't clear. At the same time, the 23-year old Masterson became friendly with Brennan and got permission from the owner of the Lady Gay to entertain her after the place closed.

Just after midnight, someone pounded at the locked door of the Lady Gay. Masterson, perhaps thinking it was friend looking for an after-hours drink, opened the door only to be confronted with a raging Melvin King brandishing his six-gun. King barged through the door. The woman screamed at him and stepped in front of Bat. King fired and the bullet tore into Mollie Brennan's stomach and she died minutes later. Either the same bullet or a different one drilled into Bat's pelvis. Somehow, he managed to draw his gun before collapsing and returned fire. The bullet struck King in the heart. A local doctor examined Bat but gave him little chance of surviving. Bat's friends, however, sent him to the army post for a physician who removed the slug and nursed him back to health. Eight weeks later, he got back in the saddle.

Masterson, a frequent visitor to Sweetwater, had the reputation of an excellent marksman but only for his buffalo hunting accomplishments. Masterson emerged from the Sweetwater Shootout with the unenviable reputation of a gunman, a reputation spent the rest of his life trying to downplay. Despite the stories crediting with gunning down many others, Melvin King turned out to be Masterson's only victim. Masterson left Texas for Dodge City, Kansas, where he served as a deputy marshal for Wyatt Earp.

He eventually ended up in New York City in the early 1900s where he worked as US Deputy Marshal, and sports editor of *The Morning Telegraph*.

FIVE

BROKEN
BUT NOT BURIED

B Y ANY STRETCH OF THE IMAGINATION, JACK SLADE SHOULD HAVE BEEN DEAD AND BURIED. HE LAY IN THE DIRT BLEEDING FROM SIX BULLET WOUNDS AND TWO SHOTGUN BLASTS. BUT HE DIDN'T DIE.

Slade worked in the high plains of Colorado as a stationmaster for Ben Holladay's Overland Stage Company. He took over the Julesburg Division after Holladay fired supervisor Jules Beni, whom he suspected of cheating him. Soon after he got the job, Slade rode out to the Beni ranch to retrieve a few horses and mules that belonged to the company. When he dismounted and headed for the ranch house, Beni stepped out and emptied his six-gun into him. While Slade writhed on the ground in pain, Beni went back into the house, grabbed his shotgun and fired both barrels at the wounded Slade. Beni ordered the stage line employee who rode along with Slade to take his boss back to the station and bury him.

Beni should have made sure Jack Slade was dead. And buried. Miraculously, he survived. Bandaged and broken, he later boarded a stagecoach for his boyhood home in Carlyle, Illinois, where he planned to recuperate. When Slade got back on his feet, Holladay rehired Slade to supervise the Rocky Ridge Division in Colorado. Once back on the job, Slade learned Beni, the man who tried to kill him, now headed-up an outlaw gang causing trouble for the stage line.

In late August 1861, Slade recruited a posse to track down the back-shooter. According to various accounts, Slade caught up with Beni and hauled him back to station headquarters where he tied him to a post and left. Slade returned the next morning with gun in hand. He took aim at Beni and fired. The bullet slammed into Beni's arm, but the shot wasn't fatal. One account says Slade took a break, ate breakfast, and returned. He shot Beni again, causing another flesh wound.

This slow, deliberate, and painful execution process continued throughout the day. In the long shadows of a setting sun, Beni finally emptied his lungs of his last breath. Beni's death didn't end the revenge. Slade pulled a knife and sliced off both ears of the outlaw and carried them around as souvenirs. Slade helped bring law and order to two divisions of the Overland Stage Company, but a taste for alcohol began clouding his judgment and behavior. In one of his drunken rages, Slade dismantled a sutler's store at Fort Halleck. The incident, and others, cost him his job.

Slade and his wife moved to the mining boomtown of Virginia City in the Montana Territory where he tried his hand at ranching. But gambling and drinking took priority along with fistfights and general rowdiness. Slade even got the blame for several robberies although there was no proof he committed them.

On March 10, 1864, a group of vigilantes took Slade into custody after he assaulted a milkman. They slipped a noose around his neck, lifted him on to a packing box, and lynched him. His wife, Virginia, took his body to Salt Lake City where she buried him but never revealed the location of his grave. Years later, authorities discovered a tombstone that read *I.A. Slade*, rather than *J. A. Slade*.

Jack Slade remains one of the mysterious and misunderstood figures of the American West. Dan Rottenberg, in his *Death of a Gunfighter: The Quest for Jack Slade, the West's Most Elusive Legend*, explores the myths and legends of Jack Slade in an effort to paint a fair portrait of the gunman.

SIX

A MAN OF UNCOMMON COURAGE

A GLIMMERING SATURDAY MORNING SUNRISE SERVED AS THE BACKDROP FOR A LARGE BAND OF KIOWA, CHEYENNE, AND COMANCHE INDIANS SWEEPING ACROSS THE PLAINS TOWARD THE ADOBE WALLS TRADING POST.

Behind the walls of the small settlement along the Canadian River in the Texas Panhandle crouched a group of buffalo hunters. The twenty eight men and one woman braced their weapons to meet the attack by an overwhelming force of war painted warriors, under the command of Quanah Parker and Isa-tai. Among those inside the compound were 23-year old William "Billy" Dixon, who served as a civilian scout, and 20-year old Bat Masterson. "The number of Indians…has been…estimated at from 700 to 1,000," wrote Dixon in his autobiography. "I believe 700 would be a safer guess."

The battle started June 27, 1874, and dragged on for several days with the defenders repelling repeated attacks. In addition to superior weapons, the hunters took cover behind the thick adobe walls and barriers they made by piling up sacks of flour and grain. Losses were put at about four. Estimates put the number of Indian losses at possibly seventy, with many more wounded, including Parker. On the third day of the confrontation, a group of about fifteen Indians waited on horseback on the side of a bluff, east of Adobe Walls Creek, about three-quarters of a mile, roughly 1,320 yards. Dixon, using a Sharps "Big Fifty" buffalo rifle, took aim and fired, toppling one of the Indians from his horse.

"A number of exaggerated accounts have been written about this incident," Dixon wrote, suggesting the shot may have resulted from more luck than skill. "I was admittedly a good marksman, yet this was what might be called a scratch shot."

After hunters in the area learned of the attack and rode into to stand alongside the others, the raiding force called it quits and left. The confrontation is known as the Second Battle of Adobe Walls. The First Battle of Adobe Walls took place ten years earlier when an estimated three thousand Kiowa, Comanche, and Plains Apache tangled with over three-hundred Army troops under Kit Carson. Dixon, later than year, fought in the Battle of Buffalo Wallow, where he and other troopers fought off a large force of hostile Indians. The battle earned Dixon the Medal of Honor, one of only eight civilians to do so.

Born September 25, 1860, in Ohio County, Virginia, Dixon later moved to Hutchinson County, Texas, to serve as sheriff, postmaster, and justice of the peace. He died March 19, 1913, at the age of 82 in Cimarron County, Oklahoma.

SEVEN

A CASE OF RETRIBUTION

BEN THOMPSON HAD HIS FILL OF THREATS BEING MADE AGAINST HIS LIFE BY A COUPLE OF THEATER OWNERS IN SAN ANTONIO, TEXAS, AND DECIDED TO CONFRONT THEM.

On the night of March 11, 1884, Thompson met up with rancher and gunman King Fisher, also the deputy sheriff of Uvalde County, Texas. The two men went to dinner and attended a play, then decided to head to the Vaudeville Variety Theater, one of San Antonio's popular gambling spots. Thompson wanted to have it out with theater owners Joe Foster and Billy Simms, who had been bad-mouthing him over a shooting two years previous. In 1882, Thompson shot and killed gambler and politician Jack Harris over a card game. Harris and Simms co-owned the Vaudeville. At the time of the shooting, Thompson was serving as City Marshal of Austin. Although he was tried and acquitted in a San Antonio court, Thompson returned to Austin and resigned his post.

When Thompson and Fisher arrived at the theater, they met with Simms, had a cordial conversation and were joined by Jacob Coy, a local lawman. Around midnight, all four were invited upstairs to meet with Foster. When they sat down in the theater box, Sims and Coy stepped away. At that moment, gunfire exploded from another theater box. Thompson and Fisher went down in a hail of bullets.

When Thompson fell, Coy—or Foster—approached and shot him in the head with a pistol. Thompson managed to squeeze off two shots in the bedlam, but died seconds later. Fisher got off one round, but took thirteen bullets to the body. No one was arrested or tried for the two killings. Thompson died at age 41. Fisher was 30.

Born in England, Ben Thompson and his family moved to Texas, in 1852, when he was nine. At that point, he began to pursue a life of high adventure, punctuated by a series of triumphs and tragedies. As a teen-ager, Thompson worked for several Austin newspapers, learning the printer's trade. But he discovered a talent for gambling and took to the road. He killed his first man in New Orleans when he was 17 over a card game. Three years later, he joined the Confederate Army in Texas, but saw little combat. After the war, Thompson left Texas, traveled to Mexico and joined Emperor Maximillian's forces.

When he returned to the Lone Star State, he got word that his sister was a victim of abuse by her husband, Jim Moore. Thompson attacked his brother-in-law, shooting him in the ribs. He was sentenced to serve four years at the Texas State Penitentiary at Huntsville, but released two years later. His next stop was Abilene, Kansas, where he opened the Bull's Head Saloon with his partner, Philip Coe. After Coe was killed in a shoot-out with Abilene Sheriff

Wild Bill Hickok, Thompson—and Wild Bill—left town, but went their own ways.

Thompson moved on to Ellsworth, Kansas, with his brother Billy. But when Billy killed Ellsworth Sheriff Chauncey Whitney, the two brothers were chased out of Kansas. Several years later, Thompson moved to Fort Elliott in the Texas Panhandle and managed to save Bat Masterson's life in a dispute over a woman.

In 1881, the citizens of Austin elected him city marshal, where he proved most effective. During his ten months as marshal, there were no murders, no burglaries and not one assault in the city.

EIGHT

DUEL
TO THE DEATH

I N THE LATE AFTERNOON OF JULY 21, 1865, A MAN WEARING A PAIR OF 1851 NAVY COLTS STRAPPED TO HIS WAIST, IVORY HANDLES TURNED FORWARD, WALKED ALONG A STREET IN SPRINGFIELD, MISSOURI, HEADING FOR THE TOWN SQUARE.

The flat broad-brimmed hat he wore cast a shadow across the gray eyes and long, droopy mustache that belonged to James Butler Hickok. Approaching the square from the south, he reached across his six-foot-three frame, pulled out one of the Colts, cocked it, and returned it the holster.

Across the square, in the distance, stood gambler Davis Tutt, an ex-Confederate soldier. The two men had traded bitter words the night before during a poker game at the Lyon House. Tutt, at one point, claimed Hickok owed him money from a previous wager and grabbed Hickok's prized gold-cased Waltham Repeater pocket watch as collateral. He threatened to wear it in public to show that Hickok didn't pay his debts. Tutt's action enraged Hickok and the two men continued arguing.

"I intend wearing it in the morning," Tutt said.

"If you do, I'll shoot you, and I warn you not to come across the square with it on," Hickok replied.

The two men stood in the town square sideways, separated by about seventy-five yards, the sun low in the sky.

"Dave, here I am. Don't you come across here with that watch," Hickok again warned him.

The two men drew. Each fired a single bullet at about the same time, according to witnesses. Tutt missed. Hickok didn't. The round from Hickok's pistol drilled into Tutt's ribs.

"Boys, I'm killed," Tutt cried out, staggering around for a few seconds before he collapsed and died.

The confrontation between Hickok and Tutt represented one of the few-recorded instances on the American frontier involving a one-on-one duel to the death. Hickok was charged with murder the next day, but it was subsequently changed to manslaughter and the case went to trial. On August 6th, the jury deliberated about "an hour or two," and acquitted him.

Hickok, better known as *Wild Bill*, had made his way to the plains of Kansas from Troy Grove, Illinois, where he was born in 1837. At age 20, he was elected constable of Monticello, Kansas, in 1855. The so-called legend of Wild Bill Hickok got its start at Rock Creek Station, Nebraska, which served as a stop for overland stagecoaches and a Pony Express station. David McCanles owned the place. He sold it to Russell, Waddell, and Majors of the Pony Express. The station had fallen on tough economic times— close to bankruptcy, in fact—and couldn't pay McCanles, who showed up at the station with his cousin James Wood and ranch hand James Gordon.

Wild Bill had just arrived in the middle of a heated argument between McCanles and Horace Wellman who operated the station. Depending on which story is told, Wild Bill apparently stepped into the bitter exchange and ended up shooting and killing McCanles from inside the house. He also wounded Woods and Gordon. Wellman, or his wife, beat the wounded Woods to death with a hoe. A shotgun blast by Hickok, or Wellman, finished off Gordon.

During a subsequent trial, Hickok and Wellman filed a plea of self-defense. As employees of the Overland Stage Company, one of the most powerful companies west of the Mississippi, the two men had plenty of influential friends at their backs. Hickok and Wellman were exonerated and, from that point, the legend grew thanks to an ambitious writer who exaggerated the story to the level and accuracy of a dime novel.

NINE

BRING 'EM IN DEAD, NOT ALIVE

WHEN US MARSHAL EVETT DUMAS NIX WALKED INTO JUDGE FRANK DALE'S OFFICE, HE COULD TELL FROM THE LOOK ON THE MAN'S FACE THAT HE HAD SOMETHING IMPORTANT TO SAY.

Square-jawed and thin-lipped Chief Justice Dale of the Oklahoma Territory Supreme Court wore a somber expression as he motioned the lawman to a chair in front of the desk.

"Marshal," he said, "I have reached the conclusion that the only good outlaw is a dead one. I hope you will instruct your deputies to bring in dead outlaws in the future. This will simplify your problem and probably save lives."

The remark took the marshal, also known as E.D. Nix, by surprise. He nodded to the judge, indicating his understanding. In his own mind, he began formulating a plan to carry out Dale's welcomed, but questionable, judicial advice.

Born September 19, 1861, in Kentucky, the son of a Confederate Army officer, Nix was no stranger to the law. His father served as a deputy sheriff and his uncle a county sheriff. After spending a few years in business operating grocery and hardware stores, Nix headed for Oklahoma during the Land Rush of 1891 where he opened a business in Guthrie.

On July 1, 1893, the Oklahoma businessman won appointment to the post of US Marshal. At 32, Nix became the youngest man holding such a position. He happened to pin on the marshal's badge in difficult and turbulent times. The Doolin Gang had been terrorizing southern Kansas and the Oklahoma Territory, robbing banks, trains, and stagecoaches, accumulating a stash of about $165,000.

A couple of years before Nix accepted the appointment, outlaw Bill Doolin teamed up with the infamous Dalton Gang, considered the "most cold-blooded robbers in the West." As luck would have it, though, Doolin decided not to participate in the gang's attempt to rob two banks simultaneously at Coffeyville, Kansas, on October 5, 1892—an attempt survived only by Emmett Dalton. At that point, Doolin formed his own gang.

Nix assembled a force of over a hundred elite field deputies that included Chris Madsen, Heck Thomas, and Bill Tilghman, better known as the *Three Guardsmen.* Over the next few years, the US Marshals Service managed to bring down the Doolin Gang. Despite his success, a cloud of controversy hovered over Nix. He was dismissed from office January 24, 1896, accused of mismanaging funds. Some historians, however, contend Nix got caught up in a fee system that was used at the time to pay officers of the US Marshals Service.

During his three years at US Marshal, Nix and his deputies killed 47 outlaws and made hundreds of arrests. Under a law on the books since 1790, the US Marshal carried out death sentences imposed by federal courts. As more death sentences were handed down, several districts installed permanent equipment. Nix, according to the US Marshals Service, carried a portable scaffold.

In 1914, Nix and Tilghman formed a film company and produced a documentary called *The Passing of Oklahoma Outlaws,* in which Nix starred along with several former deputies. He also wrote a book entitled *Oklahombres, Particularly the Wilder Ones.* Nix died on February 4, 1946, in Riverside, California, at the age of 84.

TEN

THE THREE GUARDSMEN

IN THE LATE 19TH CENTURY, THE US GOVERNMENT PURCHASED TWO MILLION ACRES OF INDIAN TERRITORY AND OPENED IT TO WHITE SETTLEMENT IN 1889, BUT THE TERRITORY PROVED A BREEDING GROUND FOR CRIME AND CORRUPTION.

Over a ten-year period, three deputy US marshals pooled their resources to track down and arrest more than 300 outlaws, and killed several others. The Three Guardsmen, as they were known, took it upon themselves to establish law and order to the Indian and Oklahoma territories. The trio consisted of William "Bill" Tilghman, Henry "Heck" Thomas, and Chris Madsen.

- *Tilghman* left home at the age of fifteen to work as a buffalo hunter and claimed, that over a five-year period, he killed 12,000 buffalo. He was once accused of murdering a man in Granada, Colorado, and was almost lynched. But the charges were false. In the late 1870s, he served as deputy sheriff of Dodge City, Kansas, under Bat Masterson and, later, became marshal. For the most part, Tilghman skirted violence as a law officer and, in his career, killed only two outlaws in gunfights.

- *Thomas*, a native of Georgia, joined the Atlanta police department in 1868. Later, he opened his own detective agency before being appointed a US deputy marshal by Judge Isaac Parker at Fort Smith, Arkansas. Thomas spent his entire life as a lawman and earned a great deal of reward money for capturing dangerous lawbreakers. He was wounded six times in gunfights.

- *Madsen*, born in Copenhagen, Denmark, had served in the Danish Army and in the Foreign Legion in Algeria before traveling to the US in 1876, where he joined the US Cavalry. He spent 14 years as a soldier, fighting in several Indian campaigns. In 1891, he went to work as a deputy US marshal in Oklahoma.

The Three Guardsmen forged a reputation for their relentless tracking abilities, which enabled them to capture or kill several well-known lawbreakers. Among the most infamous:

- *The Dalton Gang.* Emmett Dalton pointed to Heck Thomas as one of the reasons the gang tried to rob two banks simultaneously in Coffeyville, Kansas. Gang members were eager to make one last score so they could leave the territory. But Coffeyville residents resisted the robberies and killed most of the gang.

- *Wild Bunch, or Doolin Gang.* This group included surviving members of the Dalton Gang. The Three Guardsmen succeeded in killing gang members who resisted them, and arrested the others. Thomas gunned down gang leader Bill Doolin. Tilghman killed gang member William F. "Little Bill" Raidler. Madsen headed up the posse that tracked down and killed gang members "Dynamite" Dan Clifton and Richard "Little Dick" West.

⚬≫⚬

After doing their part to establish law and order, the Three Guardsmen moved on. Madsen and Heck Thomas retired in 1905. Madsen lived until 93 and died in 1944. A couple of years after Thomas retired, he took the job as police chief of Lawton, Oklahoma, but died in 1912 of Bright's Disease.

Tilghman called it quits in 1910 and was elected to the Oklahoma State Senate. He then took the job as marshal of Cromwell, Oklahoma, a wild town rife with corruption and organized crime. A corrupt politician by the name of Wiley Lynn killed him in 1924. Tilghman was 70. A month after Tilghman died, the entire town of Cromwell was burned to the ground, but no investigation was every conducted. The fire destroyed every brothel, pool hall, and flophouse throughout the town. It's believed that Chis Madsen and other friends of Tilghman ignited the blaze, but no investigation was ever conducted. The town never recovered from its wild past. Today, its population is less than 300.

The Three Guardsmen were inducted into the Oklahoma Law Enforcement Museum and *Hall of Fame* in 2009.

ELEVEN

AGAINST ALL ODDS

ON NOVEMBER 20TH, 1875, A QUASI-MILITARY BRANCH OF THE TEXAS RANGERS INVADED LAS CUEVAS, MEXICO, TO TAKE BACK CATTLE STOLEN FROM TEXAS RANCHES.

After spending three days on the southern bank of the Rio Grande, Mexican authorities relented and returned the stolen cattle. The raid was carried out by Leander Harvey McNelly as part of his mission to establish law and order to the Nueces Strip in southwest Texas, and put a stop to guerrilla operations carried out against local ranchers. The invasion serviced notice that thieves weren't safe even after they fled across the border. But, McNelly's incursion into a foreign country brought official criticism, especially in Washington, D. C. No one, however, was reprimanded.

In the years following the Civil War, bandits thundered across the Nueces River and the Rio Grande to steal cattle, loot, rape, and murder at will. The strip of land between the river and the Rio Grande served as a refuge for the lawless. Among them, Mexicans, Anglo-Americans, and marauding Indians who would herd the stolen cattle across the Rio Grande to sell. With the safety of Texas citizens at risk, Governor Richard Coke responded by turning to the Texas Rangers for help to bring law and order to the Nueces Strip. Against this backdrop emerged a special force in 1875, financed by cattle ranchers, and under the command of Captain McNelly, a master of small-unit tactics.

McNelly was born in 1844 near Follansbee, Virginia, and moved to Texas a few years later. The family moved to the Lone Star State in hopes the more arid climate would help the youngster battle *galloping consumption*, the original term for tuberculosis. Despite his health problems, McNelly joined the Fifth Texas Cavalry. He served as a Confederate officer in the Civil War, a captain in the State Police Force, and achieved the rank of captain in the Texas Rangers. When ordered by the governor to organize the special force, McNelly recruited 41 men. Even though small in number, McNelly's raiders struck with unprecedented quickness across Southwest Texas.

Despite incredible odds. The "Little McNellys," as they called themselves, faced down several Mexican bandit gangs. McNelly was the kind of leader who didn't like paperwork, and paid little attention to protocol and often disobeyed direct orders. He rarely took prisoners. And, few of his men died in battle. Despite his effectiveness, he had a reputation for conducting illegal executions and for using extreme action to force confessions from prisoners.

In early 1877, McNelly fell ill from the effects of TB he suffered from as a youth. He was forced to resign his command and retire to his farm. He died September 5, 1877, at age 33. McNelly, buried in Burton, Texas, was posthumously inducted into the Texas Ranger Hall of Fame.

TWELVE

SHOWDOWN IN DODGE CITY

TENSION FILLED THE AIR IN DODGE CITY, KANSAS, WHEN THE TRAIN CARRYING BAT MASTERSON PULLED INTO THE STATION ON THE MORNING OF APRIL 16, 1881.

Masterson made the journey from Tombstone, Arizona, when he received a telegram warning him that his younger brother Jim's life was in danger because of a business relationship gone badly.

Jim Masterson and A.J. Peacock were partners in the Lady Gay Saloon and Dance Hall. Peacock's brother-in-law, Al Updegraff, worked the place as bartender. Masterson wanted him fired for being dishonest and a drunk. Peacock refused. Threats were leveled, which prompted the telegram.

Older brother Bat, who spent the journey seething with anger, was no stranger in Dodge City. He once served as the town's sheriff, and also operated saloons and gambling houses. Wasting no time, he stepped off the train before it stopped. It was just before noon. He spotted Peacock and Updegraff in the crowded street and pushed his way through to confront them.

Guns drawn, Masterson ducked behind a railway bed. Peacock and Updegraff took cover behind the city jail. Gunshots filled the air. A few others, in support of one side or the other, joined in the shooting. One of the bullets missed Masterson, but wounded a bystander. Another bullet punctured Updegraff 's right lung.

In a matter of seconds, the sheriff and the mayor responded. Armed with shotguns, they managed to stop the shootout. Updegraff and the bystander recovered from their wounds. Mayor Ab Webster arrested Bat Masterson. Since the shooter who wounded Updegraff could not be identified, Masterson was fined eight-dollars and released. He left town that evening.

At age 27, Bat Masterson fought his last gunfight. After leaving Dodge City, he spent several years working as a lawman, saloon owner, and boxing promoter. He spent the last twenty years of his life as a newspaper columnist in New York City until he suffered a heart attack and died at his desk, October 25, 1921. The sheet of paper in his typewriter contained his last words:

> *"There are those who argue that everything breaks even in this old dump of a world of ours. I suppose these ginks who argue that way hold that because the rich man gets ice in the summer and the poor man gets it in the winter things are breaking even for both. Maybe so, but I'll swear I can't see it that way."*

THIRTEEN

BAREKNUCKLE
LAWMAN

MAINTAINING LAW AND ORDER IN ABILENE, KANSAS, IN THE LATE 1860S PROVED A CHALLENGE TOO TOUGH FOR MOST MEN. TEXAS COWBOYS SPENT MONTHS PUSHING LONGHORN CATTLE UP THE LEGENDARY CHISHOLM TRAIL INTO ABILENE FEEDLOTS WHERE THEY WOULD BE SHIPPED BY RAIL TO SLAUGHTER-HOUSES IN KANSAS CITY.

At the end of the cattle drives, drovers blew off steam by raising Cain and shooting up the place. With several thousand cowboys being paid off during a single day, city officials learned it was next to impossible to control restless cowboys with cash they wanted to spend in a town nicknamed, *Wickedest & Wildest Town in the West.*

Author Dee Brown, in *The American West*, wrote that Abilene was home to ten boarding houses, ten saloons, five general stores, and four hotels:

> "During the summer shipping season," he wrote, "the town was hot, with little swift-turning whirlwinds spinning the powdery dust in the streets. It was noisy with the continual bawling of cattle, the cries of cowhands, the dust-muffled beat of horses' hooves."

The cowboys were disrespectful of the law and openly flaunted it. A few locals volunteered to help keep the peace, but the job was simply too big. Mayor Theodore Henry even hired a couple of St. Louis police officers, but they lasted less than a day before they hopped on the eastbound train home. When construction began on a city jail, the cowboys destroyed it. Full-time, around-the-clock guards had to be assigned during the rebuilding project. Disregard for the law ran deep. When city officials published posters displaying ordinances, the cowboys would deface them with so many bullet holes there were illegible.

Tom "Bear River" Smith had once applied for the post of city marshal but was rejected. After things worsened, his application was reconsidered and he was hired. Smith arrived in Abilene on a hot, dry Saturday, June 4, 1870, to take the job as marshal for a monthly wage of $150. Lawlessness was rampant. Against this backdrop, as one of the wildest towns in the west, Smith vowed to get the situation under control.

Smith earned the nickname *Bear River* after battling a vigilante group in Bear River, Wyoming, several years previous. He also worked as a marshal in several of the Union Pacific terminal towns. Appearance-wise, the redheaded lawman looked anything but intimidating. He stood five-feet-eleven and weighed 170 pounds, but in good shape physically. Smith usually didn't carry a gun, and believed that a good lawman is one that brings lawbreakers in alive.

The first official step he took was to enforce a ban against the carrying of firearms. The firearm ban didn't sit well with the cowboys, especially Big Hank Hawkins, who boasted that no one could disarm him and live. When the inevitable face-to-face confrontation came about, the easy-mannered Smith told Hawkins he intended to enforce the law to its fullest extent. Smith, who some historians say served as a New York City policeman, traded words with Hawkins.

But the cowboy refused to disarm and told the marshal that if he wanted the guns he would have to take them. When Big Hank dropped his hand to one of the pistols, Smith stepped and sent the cowboy sprawling with a vicious uppercut.

"I will give you ten seconds to start for the city limits and get out of range," Smith said, standing over him. Big Hank picked himself up and left.

The second challenge to the firearm ban came from Wyoming Frank who held a gun on Smith, who happened to be unarmed. Smith, once a professional boxer, approached the burly cowboy, slugged him, ripped the gun away, and pistol-whipped him with it. Similar stories help define Tom Smith's legendary reputation.

Before year's end, however, Smith was shot and nearly decapitated. He died, not at the hands of cowboys, but by a couple of farmers about 12 miles outside Abilene, the wild town he tamed in less than half-a-year.

FOURTEEN

QUICK AND DEADLY

ON A RAINY SUMMER NIGHT IN 1880, TWO MEN LEFT DEADWOOD, SOUTH DAKOTA, IN A WAGON HEADED FOR ROCKERVILLE, ABOUT FIFTY MILES AWAY.

One of the men, Ambrose Bierce, manager of the Black Hills Placer Mining Company, carried $30,000 in company money stuffed in his pockets. A shotgun messenger by the name of D. Boone May sat next to him. Bierce, fearful of road agents in the area, hired May to ride along for protection. May worked for the Cheyenne and Black Hills stage line. The company hired him and other sharpshooters as stagecoach guards in hopes of putting a stop to a series of robberies by road agents. Bierce went to work for the troubled mining enterprise only as a favor to a friend who served as the company's lawyer. Bierce, a journalist, had a working knowledge of topography and engineering and a reputation as a problem-solver.

The journey to Rockerville crossed a rock rocky trail scarcely visible in the steady drizzle. May wore a rubber poncho, hunched over with his Winchester in a leather case propped up between his knees. In the black of night, May and Bierce heard the sound of a horse gaining on them from behind.

"Throw your hands up," yelled the rider.

As Bierce coaxed the team to a halt, he reached for his revolver. May reacted without hesitation. He pushed himself backward across the seat, landed upright with rifle in-hand, and fired. The bullet struck the road agent in the chest. Astonished by the incident, Bierce later wrote about May's actions, describing them as "the quickest movement that I had ever seen in anything but a cat…" When Bierce hired May, the gunman was under indictment for shooting and killing a prisoner who tried to escape his custody. He turned himself in, eventually stood trial and won acquittal.

The seventh of nine children, Daniel Boone May was born in Missouri in 1852. About eight years later, the family moved to Kansas. He and his brothers grew up helping their father farm. They also learned to shoot and hunt. In 1876, May and two of his older brothers traveled to Cheyenne and opened a freight business. They did well enough that May bought a ranch between the Platte River and Deadwood, then part of the Dakota Territory. A year later, the Cheyenne and Black Hills Stage and Express Company hired him as a shotgun messenger.

He also worked as the manager of a stage station. In a timeframe of five years, May killed at least eight robbers and took plenty of others into custody. Throughout his career, though, May got arrested on several different charges but always won his freedom. When the Black Hills gold rush slowed, May left for South America and worked as a guard at a gold mine in Chile. But, he got into trouble and left in 1891.

According to Ambrose Bierce, the sharp-eyes shootist died in South America of yellow fever.

FIFTEEN

SWEET REVENGE

NEWSPAPER EDITOR A. M. CONKLIN WAS IN A JOYFUL MOOD
WHEN HE AND HIS WIFE LEFT CHURCH AFTER THE CHRISTMAS
EVE SERVICE IN SOCORRO, NEW MEXICO.

When the couple walked down the church steps, a man stepped
out of the darkness and pulled the woman away. Another man
emerged from hiding holding a gun and fired, killing Conklin.
Earlier in the evening of December 24, 1880, Conklin found
himself in the middle of confrontation with Abran and Onofre
Baca. The brothers had been drinking and causing a disturbance.
Conklin requested they quiet down or leave. The brothers took
offense and challenged Conklin to step outside. He refused. They
left, but didn't go far. Minutes later, they gunned him down.

Efforts to track down the Baca brothers and bring them to justice dragged into the New Year. That's when a friend of Conklin,

Texas Ranger James B. Gillett, got involved. He enlisted the help of George Lloyd to pursue the killers. With a $500 reward offered for each of the brothers, the rangers tracked them to Ysleta, Texas, and the home of county judge Jose Baca, the brothers' uncle. When Gillett and Lloyd arrived, the judge offered a bribe of $1,000 to free his nephews.

"There was not enough money in El Paso County to buy me off," Gillett wrote in his autobiography, *Six Years with the Texas Rangers, 1875-1881.*

It was not until the rangers returned to New Mexico with their killers, that they realized only Abran was the brother in custody; the second man turned out to be a cousin who had nothing to do with the Conklin murder. An informant revealed to Gillett that *Onofre* Baca was working in a store in Zaragosa, Mexico. Trying to capture Baca posed a high-risk gamble. First, Gillett would be in violation of international law once he and Lloyd crossed the Rio Grande into Mexico without authorization. Furthermore, Gillett knew from experience the danger involved. He and Lloyd would have only minutes to carry out the mission. Despite the odds, they headed for Zaragosa.

Once inside the store where Baca worked, Gillett said, "I shoved my pistol up against his head and ordered him to step lively." They left the town on a dead run. A couple of miles outside Zaragosa, a Mexican posse suddenly appeared and gave chase, guns blazing. But, the pursuit ended once the two lawmen and their prisoner crossed the river into Texas. All hell broke loose once they returned to camp because Gillett and Lloyd had taken the law into their own hands. Gillett escorted Baca to Socorro, the site of the murder, and jailed the accused. Residents paid Gillett a $250 reward. But there would be no trial. Later, an angry mob stormed the jail, dragged Baca out and lynched him.

During his six years with the Texas Rangers, Gillett had patrolled mostly the West Texas border region and was involved in a number of skirmishes involving Apache, Kiowa, and Comanche Indians. His battles with Indians and the frequent pursuits of little known outlaws helped contribute to his legendary status in the rangers. But the Baca case proved his undoing. The arrest and kidnap triggered protests by the Mexican government, which pressured Texas Governor Oran M. Roberts into forcing Gillett to resign.

After he left the Texas Rangers, Gillett served as deputy marshal of El Paso in June 1882, under infamous gunman Dallas Stoudenmire. When Stoudenmire resigned after several incidents involving a hot temper and excessive drinking, Gillett pinned the badge on and became the new city marshal. When his law enforcement days came to an end, Gillett turned rancher and author, publishing a memoir that was condensed into a textbook in 1928 and used by students in at least seventeen states over a number of years.

He died of heart failure on June 11, 1937. Gillett is a member of the Texas Ranger Hall of Fame.

SIXTEEN

SHOWDOWN
AT SUNDOWN

I T WAS AROUND TWILIGHT WHEN THE TWO LAWMEN WALKED
THROUGH THE DOORWAY OF THE LOW ADOBE STRUCTURE AND
FOUND THEMSELVES FACE-TO-FACE WITH ONE OF THE MOST
FEARED BANDITS IN CALIFORNIA'S SAUSALITO VALLEY.

Juan Soto, dubbed the *Human Wildcat*, sat at a table in the shadows, surrounded by about a dozen gang members. Shadows danced across the walls from a low fire. A raw winter wind pushed through an open window. Three days earlier, Soto and his men stormed a general store in Sunol, looted the place, and killed a clerk.

Alameda County Sheriff Harry Morse led a six-man posse in January 1871 on a relentless manhunt for the brutal Soto, wanted for robbery and murder. Once inside the adobe hut, Morse drew his gun and ordered Deputy Tom Winchell to handcuff the bandit. Winchell, who never faced such odds, panicked and fled from the room when Soto's Mexican compatriots drew their own weapons. A man and a woman behind Morse grabbed his arms, but he wrenched away as Soto, gun-in-hand, scrambled to his feet and ran out the front door. In the growing darkness, Morse fired and drilled a bullet through Soto's hat.

The outlaw turned and squeezed off four bullets at the sheriff. They all missed. Exasperated, he rushed Morse. The sheriff broke into a run for his horse to retrieve his rifle and, on the way, snapped off a shot from his revolver that jammed Soto's gun. Soto ran back inside the building, grabbed several guns, and ran to one of the tethered horses. But the horse bolted and Soto headed for cover on foot. Morse slid the .44 caliber Winchester from his saddle sheath, aimed, and pulled the trigger. The bullet raced 150 yards and ripped into Soto's shoulder, knocking him to the ground. Wounded and bleeding, Soto struggled to his feet, screaming at Morse. Wild with rage, the bandit charged across the meadow toward Morse. But the lawman calmly took aim. The next bullet struck Soto in the head and he fell to the ground, dead.

The news of Morse's courageous showdown with Soto traveled throughout California earning him praise "as one of the most daring and desperate acts that have ever been formed in the history of detective work on the Pacific Coast…" Although Morse's persistence of tracking, capturing, or killing dangerous outlaws attracted the respect of fellow lawmen, his achievements often escaped widespread attention. Most of the publicity of the era went to his contemporaries—such men as Wild Bill Hickok, Wyatt Earp, and Bat Masterson.

He retired as sheriff in 1878, and opened a detective agency in San Francisco. In 1883, he was credited with the arrest of Charles Bowles, better known as Black Bart, who robbed a number of stagecoaches. Morse died of natural causes at 76 in 1912.

SEVENTEEN

LONG, HOT, VIOLENT SUMMER

IN THE SUMMER OF 1884, A GROUP OF ANGRY RANCHERS WHO CALLED THEMSELVES *STUART'S STRANGLERS* SWEPT ACROSS CENTRAL MONTANA KILLING CATTLE RUSTLERS AND HORSE THIEVES.

These outlaws proved an incessant problem across the Plains in the 1880s, but especially in Montana. The state's wide-open spaces accommodated more heads of cattle than people. Well-organized gangs of rustlers operated throughout the sparsely populated country much as they pleased because of a lack of law enforcement. At first, the cattlemen couldn't agree on how to deal with the problem. Most were opposed to any direct confrontation, primarily because of the outlaws' superior firepower and experience. When the rustlers heard about the cattlemen's indecision, they stepped up their rustling activities.

Frustrated at the inability of local law enforcement authorities to take appropriate action, rancher Granville Stuart and fourteen other cattle ranchers met in secret and outlined a plan to take the law into their own hands. The newly formed Vigilante Committee had one goal: Putting a stop to brazen cattle rustlers and horse thieves operating out of the Missouri Breaks.

During the long, hot, and violent summer, the Stranglers carried out a mission with no mercy. They killed more than twenty rustlers and thieves. Some died in gunfights. Others were executed, their bodies swinging from ropes identified with place cards that read either "Horse Thief" or "Cattle Thief." According to one newspaper account, July 26, 1884, the Stranglers "have hanged or shot thirteen of the offenders within three weeks, five being captured and hanged at Rocky Point on the upper Missouri River." A few days later, a Helena newspaper reported, "Fully fifty thieves were hanged or shot in the past month."

As the retribution continued, Stuart came under severe criticism for his actions, mostly from lawmen. But Stuart never apologized. In fact, he assumed full responsibility for the attacks against the rustlers. The Montana Stock Growers' Association showed its appreciation by electing him president that same summer. Stuart wore many hats during his 84 years of living. His list of accomplishments is unparalleled among those who helped settle the American frontier. In addition to pioneer, prospector, and cattleman, he also served as an author, civic and business leader, and diplomat.

Born in Clarksburg, Virginia, (now West Virginia) in 1834, his family moved to Illinois and then Iowa. At eighteen, he and his brother James traveled to California with their father to prospect for gold. The trio then settled in Deer Lodge Valley in Western Montana, in 1857. The pair received credit for making the first major gold strike in Montana. Over the years, Stuart bought and sold a mercantile business, served as a bookkeeper for the First National Bank in Helena, and then got into the cattle business with two other men, forming the DHS Ranch in 1879. Four years later, Stuart enjoyed a tidy profit for his company, ranging about 12,000 shorthorns.

During the fall roundup, however, he determined that cattle rustlers had taken about three percent of the herd. When he learned other cattle ranchers experienced the same kinds of losses, Stuart invited them to meet in secrecy and organized *Stuart's Stranglers*.

After the disastrous winter of 1886-87, Stuart left the cattle business. President Grover Cleveland appointed him ambassador to Paraguay and Uruguay in 1894. He died at Missoula, Montana, Oct. 2, 1918.

EIGHTEEN

A LAWMAN FEARED & RESPECTED

THE MAN WEARING THE BADGE ADJUSTED THE BANDANA SO IT COVERED THE BACK OF HIS NECK TO PROTECT IT FROM THE HEAT. HE WAS TIRED, SADDLE SORE, AND A FEW DAYS FROM TURNING 46, BUT WASN'T ABOUT TO LET EXCUSES STAND BETWEEN HIM AND THE MAN HE WAS HUNTING.

Orlando "Rube" Robbins had spent part of July and August 1882 tracking escaped prisoner Charley Chambers across the Dakota Territory into the Oregon Territory, most of it under a scorching sun. The marshal finally captured the convicted robber in Portland and returned him to prison in Boise—completing a 1,280-mile journey. But, Robbins was unlike other men. If fact, many of his contemporaries referred to him as the "man most responsible for bringing law and order to the Idaho Territory."

Robbins, born in Maine, left home at 17 following a quarrel with his father and made his way to the California gold fields for a short while. In his mid-20s moved to Idaho after the discovery of gold in the Salmon River area. He got an early start in law enforcement when he was appointed deputy sheriff in 1864. When Sheriff Sumner Pinkham got defeated in the next election, Robbins joined a stagecoach line where he rode shotgun to discourage robberies.

His success at dealing with the outlaw element helped him sustain a long career in law enforcement. Twenty-five of those years were spent as deputy US Marshal under several different marshals. Appointed in 1865, Robbins also served as the police chief of Boise, Ada County Sheriff, and warden at the Idaho State Penitentiary. Robbins also won election to the Idaho Legislature from Ada County twice and somehow found the time to broaden his list of accomplishments.

As a colonel in the Idaho militia, Robbins served as a successful scout and Indian-fighter, part of the command that followed the fleeing Nez Perce across the mountains of Idaho. The lawman also became something of a local hero for his role in the Bannock War of 1878, managing to survive several close encounters with death. He owned a cattle ranch where he also raised blooded race horses and also founded a temperance lodge in Ada County.

Robbins feared no one, a point that was illustrated by the editors of *True West Magazine*, in "True Tales and Amazing Legends of the Old West." According to the story, a group of confederate sympathizers, who gathered in a local saloon on July 4, 1864, vowed they wouldn't tolerate any Yankee singing "The Star Spangled Banner" during the day. It took place just before Robbins became town deputy. Robbins who hadn't yet been deputized, walked into the saloon, climbed atop a billiard table to get everyone's attention and drew his two pistols. As he glared at the crowd, he sang the song in a loud voice, holstered the pistols, jumped down to the floor and left.

No one said or did anything.

The well-respected lawman, considered the toughest in Idaho, died on May 1, 1908, of a heart attack. He was 72. At the time, he was still on the job, working as a traveling guard for prisoners. An impressive monument to him was erected in Pioneer Cemetery in Boise. And a tribute at the cemetery's website carries this quote from an early state historian:

"He was feared, yet respected by every bad man and 'gun-fighter' who ever sojourned in Idaho, and it is doubtful if any officer made more arrests of that class than he."

NINETEEN

BOOZE, BULLETS, & BRAVERY

IN THE AFTERNOON OF NOVEMBER 5, 1877, ACCUSATIONS OVER MONEY TRIGGERED A LOUD QUARREL INSIDE THE LONE STAR DANCE HALL IN DODGE CITY, KANSAS, PROMPTING ONE OF THE CUSTOMERS TO SUMMON DEPUTY MARSHAL ED MASTERSON.

When Masterson stormed through the doors, he saw a man by the name of Bob Shaw leveling a gun at Texas Dick Moore, who owned the Lone Star. The drunk and disorderly Shaw accused Moore of stealing forty dollars from him. Masterson ordered Shaw to give up his gun. He refused and took a shot at Moore. Masterson walked up and clubbed Shaw over the head with the butt on his six-gun. Shaw shook off the blow, whirled, and fired.

The ball hit the lawman's right breast, struck a rib, and came out under the right shoulder blade, paralyzing his right arm. After his gun hit the floor, Masterson dropped to his knee, retrieved the six-shooter with his left hand and returned fire. The shots hit Shaw in the left arm and left leg, knocking him off his feet. A random bullet struck Moore in the groin, a wound from which he eventually recovered. According to the November 10, 1877, issue of the *Dodge City Times*:

"…The nerve and pluck displayed by officer Masterson reflects credit both upon himself and the city, which has reason to congratulate itself upon the fact that it has a guardian who shirks no responsibility and who hesitates not to place himself in danger when duty requires."

A few months later, city officials promoted Masterson to city marshal.

A little before 10 pm, on the night of April 9, 1878, the marshal and Deputy Nat Haywood walked into the Lady Gay saloon where a half-dozen cowboys stood at the bar, celebrating. One of them, Jack Wagner, carried a pistol, a direct violation of the city's gun ordinance. Rather than make a scene, Masterson quietly disarmed Wagner and handed the gun to Wagner's boss, A.M. Walker. He and Haywood left. Walker, who consumed his own share of booze during the evening, handed Wagner's gun back to him. The two decided to go after Masterson and his deputy.

What started as a shoving match and fistfight turned something more deadly. Wagner's gun went off. The bullet tore through the marshal's belly and came out his lower back. Bleeding, with his coat on fire from the flash of gunpowder, Masterson somehow found the strength to pull his own gun and fired four times. One bullet found Wagner's stomach. The other three hit Walker. Wagner stumbled into a nearby Peacock Saloon, collapsed, and died the next day. Masterson, coat still on fire, staggered across the plaza, crossed the tracks, and walked into George M. Hoover's saloon. Several customers carried him to Bat's room upstairs. But, the wounds were too serious. Surrounded by friends and his brother, Ed died about thirty minutes later.

The popular and highly-respect lawman was only 26.

TWENTY

SMALL MAN WITH BIG COURAGE

JOHN HORTON SLAUGHTER HAD HARD BLACK EYES THAT COULD STARE A HOLE RIGHT THROUGH A MAN. SITTING AT A POKER TABLE ON COMMERCE STREET IN SAN ANTONIO IN 1876, HE WATCHED THE LAST HAND DEALT.

Minutes later, Barney Gallagher slammed his hole card down and claimed victory. When he reached for the winnings, he found himself staring into the barrel of Slaughter's a six-shooter. "Those cards have been marked," Slaughter said. "The money stays here." Gallagher, a man with the reputation as a cattle rustler, denied the accusation, hurled a few loud threats, and stalked out. A showdown was inevitable.

Slaughter was born in Louisiana on Oct. 2, 1841. He built an enviable resume of accomplishments throughout his life. He stood only five-feet, six inches. But, his single-mindedness, and skill with guns, made him a lot taller in the eyes of his enemies. Slaughter's colorful career spanned one of the roughest eras in the history of the American frontier. He worked as a Texas Ranger after the Civil War. While building a reputation as a prominent cattle rancher, he also spent time as a professional gambler.

In 1886, Slaughter got elected sheriff of Arizona's outlaw-ridden Cochise County. Texas John Slaughter, as he was also known, won admiration as the last courageous lawmen in Arizona history. He earned the praise of Wild Bill Hickok, Wyatt Earp, Sam Bass, Pat Garrett, and Billy the Kid. Historians credit him, more than anyone else, with cleaning up the Arizona Territory. Slaughter assumed responsibility for bringing lawlessness under control in the Tombstone area. His tracking skills were second to none. The county consisted of six thousand square miles of desert terrain. But, he wouldn't hesitate to pursue lawbreakers. Slaughter wouldn't return from the hunt until he captured the lawbreakers. Sometimes, he found the need to resolve the situation with his gun.

The rancher logged lots of hours playing cards. In fact, he found gambling more exciting and profitable than working his ranch or chasing outlaws. His wife, Cora Viola Slaughter, threatened several times to leave him. She disliked the amount of time gambling kept him away from home. One writer described Slaughter as "the meanest good guy who ever lived."

Slaughter and Gallagher came face-to-face again to settle the dispute over the card game they once played. Historians say Gallagher tracked his poker-playing rival all the way to New Mexico. He caught up to Slaughter during a cattle drive. With a sawed-off shotgun cocked and ready, Gallagher leveled it at Slaughter who was riding toward him. According to one account, Slaughter pulled his pistol and fired, striking Gallagher in the chest or the thigh. Gallagher bled to death.

Slaughter proved a formidable businessman. He formed several cattle partnerships with his brothers. And, they drove throughout the West and Southwest. In 1892 and 1893, a major drought triggered a collapse of the cattle market, striking a financial blow to cattle ranchers. The episode forced Slaughter to mortgage his property. He retired to his San Bernardino ranch near Douglas, Arizona, and died in his sleep, Feb. 15, 1922.

TWENTY-ONE

RETRIBUTION IN LARAMIE

D ESPITE A WARNING FROM DEPUTY MARSHAL STEVE LONG, THE
EIGHT MEN CONTINUED TRADING PUNCHES IN A FULL-SCALE
STREET BRAWL IN LARAMIE, WYOMING. LONG, ANGRY HIS COM-
MAND WAS IGNORED, DREW HIS GUN, AND BEGAN FIRING. SECONDS
LATER, ON A TUESDAY AFTERNOON, OCTOBER 22, 1867, FIVE MEN
LAY IN THE DIRT, DEAD.

"Big" Steve Long, as he was known, traveled into the Dakota
Territory with his half-brothers, Ace and Con Moyer, and opened
a block-long tent saloon in Laramie named *Bell of the West*. Locals
called it the *Bucket of Blood*. Few details are available about Long's
past. It's believed he fought for the Confederacy during the Civil
War, but possibly under a different name. He drifted into Wyoming
in the mid-1860s. As Laramie's first marshal, Long—who stood six-
feet-six—established a reputation as a man of violence. Rather

than arrest anyone, he preferred to intimidate them with physical force—or outright shoot them. But, he didn't limit his abusive behavior to only matters of law enforcement.

Long, along with his half-brothers, used strong-arm tactics to force several area ranchers to sign over the deeds of their properties to them. The ones who refused were later gunned down. Long claimed he killed the men because they attempted to draw on him. If the victim had no gun at the time of the shooting, Long made sure one was found on the dead man. And, there were never any witnesses. By October 1868, Long had killed thirteen men. He was also suspected of killing another seven, although no concrete evidence existed to link him to the murders.

Laramie's first Mayor M. C. Brown, and the entire town government, called it quits in May 1868, after only three weeks in office, frustrated by threats from the three half-brothers. Brown deemed Laramie "ungovernable."

On October 18, 1868, Long tried to rob Rollie "Hard Luck" Harrison, but the local prospector refused to back down and drew his gun to defend himself. The shootout cost Harrison his life, but he had wounded Long, who fled the scene. When Long sought refuge with his fiancée and told her what happened, she later slipped away and told Sheriff Nathaniel Kimball Boswell, who organized a small posse. The men finally cornered Long and his half-brothers at the saloon on October 28 and took them into custody. The posse dragged them to an unfinished cabin behind the Frontier Hotel, where they rigged a makeshift gallows. Long asked if he could be allowed to remove his boots because, "My mother always said I'd die with my boots on."

The marshal's campaign of terror came to an end when all three were hanged from the rafters of the cabin.

TWENTY-TWO

ACCIDENTAL SHOOTING IN TOMBSTONE

N<small>O ONE VENTURED ALONG</small> T<small>OMBSTONE'S</small> A<small>LLEN</small> S<small>TREET ON THE</small> NIGHT OF O<small>CTOBER</small> 28, 1880, <small>WHERE A LOOSELY-ASSOCIATED</small> GROUP OF OUTLAWS WHO CALLED THEMSELVES THE *C<small>OWBOYS</small>* <small>KEPT THE TOWN ON EDGE BY FIRING THEIR SIX-SHOOTERS INTO THE NIGHT SKY.</small>

The reckless shooting and wild partying continued for two days until Marshal Fred White, Tombstone's first town marshal, decided to take action. White, however, figured he'd be foolish to tackle the job alone and enlisted the help of Wyatt Earp, deputy undersheriff of the Southern portion of what was then Pima County. From all accounts, the 31-year old White, who had been elected in January, was respected for his fairness and professionalism. In the previous ten months, he occasionally arrested members of the Cowboys faction, but rarely encountered any resistance. Among the Cowboys were the Clanton brothers, the McLaury brothers, and "Curly" Bill Brocious, with whom he was on particularly friendly terms.

On the second day of the shootings, White and Earp decided to approach from opposite ends of the street and sandwich the rowdy and drunken group between them. The situation worked as planned, and White managed to disarm all of them with little trouble. Later than night, White confronted Curly Bill in a vacant lot on Allen Street firing his revolver indiscriminately into the air. The marshal approached Brocious and demanded he turn over his gun. When White closed his hand over the barrel and pulled, the gun discharged. A .45 caliber bullet ripped through the marshal's left groin. Apparently, the hammer of the gun rested in a "half-cocked" position over a live round.

Earp spotted the flash of the gun in the dark, ran to help White, and hammered the butt of his own weapon against Brocious' head until he fell to the ground unconscious. Earp's brothers, Morgan and Virgil, helped get White to the doctor's office, and dragged the gunman off to jail. Brocious expressed regrets over the shooting, contending it was purely accidental, lamenting that, because of his drunken state, he didn't realize the hammer was half-cocked.

The wound wasn't considered serious at the time. The *Tombstone Epitaph* reported, "Marshal White was shot in the left groin, the ball passing nearly thru, and being cut from the buttocks by Dr. Mathews. The wound is a serious though not fatal one." Two days later, however, White passed away. Before dying, the marshal made a deathbed statement saying he believed the shooting was accidental and didn't blame Brocious. In court, his testimony was entered into evidence. At the same time, a demonstration was staged to show how Brocious' gun could have indeed fired accidentally from the half-cocked position.

At a preliminary hearing, December 27, 1880, the evidence presented was ruled insufficient to hold Curly Bill for trial. Despite the ruling, and his regret over killing the marshal, Brocious remained bitter over the pistol-whipping administered by Earp—an event that led to spiraling tensions between Earp and the Cowboys and culminated in the gunfight at the OK Corral.

White was buried in Row 6 at Boothill Graveyard in Tombstone.

TWENTY-THREE

LEGENDARY JUDGE ROY BEAN

L IKE ANY BUSINESS OWNER, ROY BEAN WANTED TO FIND A WAY TO BOOST THE PROFITS OF HIS MILK DELIVERY BUSINESS IN SAN ANTONIO. SO HE DECIDED TO ADD CREEK WATER TO THE MILK.

According to various accounts, all seemed fine until a buyer or two noticed minnows in the milk. Bean seemed equally surprised when confronted, telling customers, "By Gobs, I'll have to stop them cows from drinking out of the creek." In the spring of 1882, Bean had moved on and opened a saloon-courthouse in the barren badlands of southwestern Texas, near the Pecos River, in a tent city he named Vinegaroon, and later at nearby Langtry.

Nearly eight-thousand railroad workers lived within a twenty-mile radius, but the nearest court was about two hundred miles away. When the Texas Rangers requested local law jurisdiction for Vinegaroon, Bean managed to gain an appointment as Justice of the Peace for the new precinct in Pecos County. The saloon served as the judge's headquarters as well as the hub of an unorthodox brand of frontier justice and entrepreneurism.

The exterior of the saloon functioned as an advertising billboard. On the roof stood a sign: JUDGE ROY BEAN, NOTORY PUBLIC. Beneath it were more signs. One announced: JUSTICE OF THE PEACE. Another sign read: LAW WEST OF THE PECOS. A smaller placard, tucked under the roof, read: ICE BEER.

Inside the saloon is where Judge Roy Bean dispensed his special concoction for justice, consisting of one part commonsense, a few doses of greed and prejudice, and a generous helping of colorful behavior. For example, he once said, "Hang 'em first, try 'em later." Another quote attributed to Bean was, "I know the law...I am its greatest transgressor."

Various stories say Bean renamed his site Langtry after the self-professed love of his life, Lillie Langtry–a British actress whom he never met. A Langtry, Texas, however, already existed, named in honor of George Langtry, an engineer and foreman of the Southern Pacific who had supervised a Chinese work crew building the railroad. Apparently, Bean had squatted on part of the railroad land, and it wasn't long before his saloon attracted hundreds of railway workers. He added yet another sign to the outside of the saloon to honor the actress. It read *The Jersey Lilly*, but the sign painter misspelled her name.

The actress, while on tour, once visited Langtry to call on Bean. By the time she arrived, the judge had died. Officials presented her with his gun and *Langtry* bequeathed it to the state of Jersey in the United Kingdom. It is currently on display with a number of her personal effects in the Jersey Museum.

During his years on the bench, Roy Bean relied on one law book: the 1879 edition of the *Revised Statutes of Texas*, and never allowed revised editions to find their way to his courtroom. Bean had the power to hold inquests, perform marriages, grant divorces, and stage trial for a number of different crimes. In his courtroom, there were no such things as hung juries or appeals allowed. Jurors were expected to buy a drink during every court recess. Bean once even fined a dead man forty dollars. Since Langtry had no jail. Bean settled all cases with fines—which were made for the exact amount the defendant had in his pocket. He kept all the money; the state received nothing.

Bean charged $10 for any divorce, even though only district courts had the power to legally grant them. Weddings cost $5. Bean, incidentally, ended every wedding ceremony with the words "and may God have mercy on your souls" –traditionally used at the end of a death sentence. Bean was unorthodox, to be certain, and he proved masterful at promoting himself in such as way as to help his legendary status. And it worked.

In 1896, he promoted a heavyweight boxing championship between Bob Fitzsimmons and Peter Maher on an island in the Rio Grande, even though boxing matches were illegal in both Texas and Mexico. He arranged to stage it on the Mexican side of the river, knowing full well that Mexican authorities couldn't reach the site in time to stop it. The fight lasted one minute and thirty-five seconds but the subsequent sports coverage helped spread Roy Bean's reputation across the US.

Bean and Judge Isaac Parker of Ft. Smith, Arkansas, are sometimes confused for each other. Parker was the actual *hanging judge*. Bean never actually hanged anyone, although he occasionally "staged" hangings to scare criminals. Bean and his staff would allow for the prisoner to escape. This second chance convinced the culprits never to appear before the court again.

Judge Roy Bean died in 1903, after a drinking binge.

TWENTY-FOUR

MAKE THE FIRST SHOT THE LAST

WYATT EARP, INVOLVED IN VARIOUS SHOOTOUTS DURING HIS CAREER, ONCE TOLD AN INTERVIEWER THAT SPEED HAD NOTHING TO DO WITH SUCCESS IN A GUN BATTLE. "DELIBERATION" WAS THE KEY—TAKING THE TIME TO AIM AND PULL THE TRIGGER ONCE.

One of the few documented instances of two men facing each other in a quick-draw duel took place on July 21, 1865, in Springfield, Missouri, between Wild Bill Hickok and David Tutt because of a dispute over a card game. The two men stood sixty- to seventy-paces apart in the town square. Both fired about the same time. Tutt missed. Hickok didn't. (*Chapter 8, Duel to the Death*).

Main Street showdowns, for the most part, were rare occurrences in the Old West. In most cases, if sharp-shooting gunmen found themselves in the same locale, they'd usually stay away from each other out of respect or fear—and took few risks. Pure self-promotion accounted for most of the reputations among gunmen. Hickok, for example, helped create and perpetuate the myth of quick-draw gun battles in an interview with *Harper's New Monthly Magazine* in which he bragged that he had killed hundreds of men. Several newspapers, however, contended the article was riddled with inaccuracies.

In a 1928 interview with author Stuart N. Lake, for the book *Wyatt Earp: Frontier Marshal,* Earp mocked the image of a man holding a gun in each hand, "held closely against his hips and both spitting smoke together." He branded it as nothing more than "the picture of a fool or a fake." The gunfighters who did wear two guns, never fired them at the same time, he told Lake.

"Some men could shoot equally well with either hand, and in a gunplay might alternate their fire; others exhausted the loads from the gun on the right, or the left...then shifted the reserve weapon to the natural shooting hand...." Although a few "of these so-called two-gun men" tried shooting both guns at once, Earp pointed out they "didn't last long in proficient company."

Earp also said the idea of notching a gun was nothing more than a myth. The pros, he said, never did such a thing. "I never knew a man who amounted to anything to notch his gun with *credits*, as they were called, for men he had killed. Outlaws, gunmen of the wild crew who killed for the sake of brag, followed this custom. I have worked with most of the noted peace officers... (who) have handled their weapons many times, but never knew any of them to carry a notched gun."

The former lawman also expressed contempt for anyone would attempt to bluff another person with a gun. "There was no such thing as a bluff," Earp said, adding when a gunfighter reached for his forty-five, "every faculty he owned was keyed to shooting as speedily and as accurately as possible, to making his first shot the last of the fight."

The perception among a number of writers that Earp never liked to talk about himself was far from reality when it came to his gun fighting days. In addition to the extensive interview he gave Lake for the book, Earp also opened up about himself to several other interviewers regarding his personal achievements, especially during his days in Dodge City. In several instances, however, the stories lacked documentation or corroboration.

Lake's book mentions that Edward Judson of Stamford, New York—who wrote successful dime novels under the pen name, *Ned Buntline*—presented Earp, Bat Masterson, and three other Dodge City residents in 1876 with special-order Colt Peacemaker revolvers with extra-long barrels, dubbed the *Buntline Special.* Colt's manufacturing records make no mention of the special-order weapons. Furthermore, no reference has ever been found in Buntline's writings about the weapon, or that he ever visited Dodge City.

Lake was even accused of making up the story, but his notes reveal he got it from Earp during his interviews. According to his notes, Lake's efforts to confirm its authenticity also failed. Others, however, contend the story about the Buntline Special is true. Author William B. Shillingberg, after conducting an extensive study, published an article (1976)—*Wyatt Earp and the Buntline Special Myth*—said experts noted "the absence of any supporting evidence from pre-*Frontier Marshal* secondary sources or available primary documentation."

TWENTY-FIVE

RUFE CANNON'S PERSISTENCE

ON OCTOBER 17, 1892, US MARSHAL RUFUS CANNON RODE INTO FORT SMITH, ARKANSAS, IN OKLAHOMA TERRITORY, WITH CREEK INDIAN FUGITIVE CAPTAIN JOHN WILLIE, A CREEK INDIAN ACCUSED OF KILLING A FELLOW DEPUTY MARSHAL.

A year earlier, Captain Willie had gunned down Deputy US Marshal George Thornton in a nighttime ambush near the Sac and Fox Indian Agency. When US District Judge Isaac Parker took office in March 1875, he made it a point to recruit black men as Deputy US Marshals. Cannon was considered among the more notable black deputies in Indian Territory, although not as well-known as Bass Reeves and Grant Johnson. Cannon served as a member of the posse headed up by US Marshal Heck Thomas who killed outlaw Bill Doolin on August 24, 1896. A Guthrie, Oklahoma, newspaper reported that Cannon was the one who shot Doolin but later retracted the report, giving Thomas credit as the actual shooter.

Rufe Cannon worked the Oklahoma and Indian Territories in the 1890s and got involved in several high profile cases. On January 21, 1893, he found himself in a gunfight with Cherokee outlaw Henry Starr and his gang. Starr, and outlaws Ed Newcome and Jesse Jackson made a run for it. Two escaped, but Cannon brought down Jackson with a shotgun blast to the right arm. He was taken into custody for the November 1892 train robbery. Cannon also captured outlaw Scott Bruner in connection with the same robbery. According to *The Coffeyville Journal,* "Bruner is a desperate fellow and the capture is an important one."

An extensive manhunt got underway in July 1895 for Bob and Bill Christian, two brothers who escaped from the Oklahoma City Jail and killed Police Chief Milt Jones. After learning that William "Old Man" Christian, the father, and former lawman W.H. Carr helped stage the escape, Cannon tracked both men down before the end of the month.

Cannon, it's believed, was born in 1847 in Arkansas. He was commissioned as Deputy Marshal on September 15, 1892, according to records at the Fort Smith National Historic Site. Rufe Cannon died in Oklahoma City on October 15, 1950. He was 103.

TWENTY-SIX

THE MAN WHO TAMED SILVER CITY

T HE SUN BEGAN SLIDING BEHIND THE DISTANT HAZY BLUE MOUN-
TAIN RANGE IN SOUTHWESTERN NEW MEXICO AS ACTING SILVER
CITY MARSHAL HARVEY WHITEHILL WATCHED WORKERS AT THE
GAGE RAILROAD SIDING REMOVE TWO BODIES FROM THE WRECKAGE
OF A PASSENGER TRAIN.

The two men—engineer T.C. Webster, and messenger guard
T.G. Hodgkins—had been shot to death when four masked men
derailed and attacked the eastbound Southern Pacific in the late
afternoon of Saturday, November 24, 1883. Whitehill, on horseback, shook his head, perplexed that such a small sum of money,
$518 in coin and $312 in currency, would result in the deaths of two
men. But little surprised this veteran lawman, now on his mid-40s.

The seriousness of the crime prompted Wells Fargo, the
Southern Pacific, and the U.S. Post Office to each contribute

enough cash to push the reward total to $8,800 for the arrest and conviction of the gang. With such a tempting financial incentive at stake, Whitehill had no trouble assembling a posse of eight men who began tracking the killers. An intense manhunt, highlighted by good detective work and a bit of good luck, led Whitehill and his posse to Apache County, Arizona, in mid-January where they arrested the outlaws. Gang members were taken back to Silver City and jailed. On March 10th they escaped, but were quickly recaptured. By mid-March, three of the gang members had been either shot to death or hanged. The fourth, Christopher "Kit" Joy, was sentenced to life in prison and ended up serving twelve years.

The reward money was split among eight posse members. Whitehill and two others got $1,333 apiece. Another got $888. The fifth posse member took home $444, while the rest received $500 each.

The Wooster, Ohio native, born Sept 2, 1837, traveled to Leadville, Colorado, in the late 1850s for a gold mining adventure and reportedly took $15,000 from his claim and moved to the Southwest in 1860. Whitehill got involved in the Apache Wars of the 1860s. He wound up in New Mexico where he worked as a miner for a time, and then moved to Silver City in the 1870s, built a home, and got married.

In 1874, he ran for the post of Grant County sheriff, and won. At the time, the county seat of Silver City was considered a violent community. But Whitehill wasted no time in imposing his brand of law and order, establishing a reputation for dealing quickly with trouble. The following year, he created controversy by hiring gunman "Dangerous Dan" Tucker, to help keep the pace. Whitehill and Tucker, according to several accounts, were involved in several shootouts with outlaws and a few law-breaking miners. But the impact Whitehill and Tucker had on Silver City was permanent.

Harvey Whitehill proved to be the right man for the job of taming Silver City. Voters liked him so well that they elected him for six terms, but not consecutively. In 1882, he left the job to serve a term in the Territorial Legislature. In that same year, lawman Pat Garrett came to Silver City, with the reputation of having killed Billy the Kid. He decided to take on Whitehill for job of sheriff. Garrett, however, wasn't all that well liked, and lost to Whitehill. The campaign and election were shaded by a bit of irony.

While Garrett was the *last* person to arrest Billy the Kid, known as Henry McCarty and Henry Antrim at the time, Whitehill was the *first* to arrest him—twice—both times for theft in Silver City. The first time, Whitehill let him go with a warning. The second time, he put him behind bars, but the Kid escaped—the first prisoner to do so from Whitehill's jail.

After serving his last term, 1889-1890, Harvey Whitehill left his badge behind, having serve ten years at the post. He died in Deming, New Mexico, on September 14, 1906, at age 69. Although not as well known as other lawman of the time, historians credit Whitehill him with being far more effective than most of the others.

TWENTY-SEVEN

SHOOT FIRST, QUESTIONS LATER

H AT PULLED LOW, BLUE EYES SCANNING RIGHT AND LEFT, THE MAN WEARING THE BADGE PATROLLED THE STREETS OF DEMING, NEW MEXICO, IN LATE NOVEMBER 1881, A DOUBLE-BARREL SHOTGUN IN HIS HANDS AND A COLT ON HIS HIP.

Dan Tucker, the City Marshal of Shakespeare, New Mexico, was sent to Deming to deal with an outlaw gang that had taken control of the town. Tucker wasted no time in making his presence known. He was a man who meant business with a reputation of someone who never hesitated at pulling the trigger when the situation called for it. Gang members learned quickly why the deadly shooting skills of this visiting lawman earned him the nickname, *Dangerous Dan*.

Newspaper reporter C.M. Chase, in town to write a story about the Southern Pacific Railroad and the new railroad junction at Deming, said three days after Tucker's arrival, three of the outlaws were dead, two others wounded. By the following February, the gang had moved on and, according to the *Southwest Sentinel* of Silver City, "Everything is quiet in Deming." Although Tucker doesn't rank in name-recognition with some of the more well-known gunmen of the Old West, historian Leon C. Metz said "Tucker was a better lawman, and more dangerous, than such redoubtable characters as Wyatt Earp and Wild Bill Hickok."

Born in Canada in 1849, Tucker eventually drifted into Grant County, New Mexico, where Sheriff Harvey Whitehill hired him as a deputy in 1875. Three years later he became Silver City's first town marshal, before leaving in 1880 to take the same job at the mining camp of Shakespeare. In November 1878, his first year on the job, he was wounded during a shootout with an outlaw named Caprio Rodriguez, who tried to resist arrest. But, when the gunsmoke settled, Rodriguez lay dead.

Tucker brought law and order to the streets of Shakespeare, rounding up more than a dozen members of a cowboy gang in 1881. In September, he shot and killed a cattle rustler named Jake Bond. A couple of months later, just before leaving for Deming, he put a fatal bullet in a man who rode his horse into a local hotel dining room. The same month, he arrested outlaws Sandy King and "Russian Bill" Tattenbaum, who were hanged from the rafters inside the Grant House at Shakespeare by a band of local vigilantes.

During his law enforcement career, Tucker also served as a deputy US marshal, livestock inspector, and train agent. Tucker casts sort of an opaque shadow across the history pages of the violent frontier period of southwest New Mexico, which encompassed Grant County, Silver City, Las Cruces, Deming, and Socorro.

"For a time—50 years or so—Silver City was the stage for Wild West drama of the first order, with a cast of colorful players numbering in the hundreds. They were not actors, though, and the set was not a sham. There was nothing counterfeit about the people or the place," says Bob Alexander, author of *Dangerous Dan Tucker: New Mexico's Deadly Lawman.*

Tucker, according to various accounts, found himself in the middle of about a dozen gun battles. He didn't go in for a lot of chitchat and rarely asked questions of the men he pursued, preferring a shoot-first-ask-questions-later approach. He once admitted to the *Silver City Enterprise* that "in the course of his duty as deputy sheriff, he has been obliged to kill eight men in this county, besides several in Lincoln and Dona Ana counties" and personally escorted four others to the gallows.

In 1884, he tried his hand at business, operating the Eclipse Restaurant and Saloon in Deming, but the following year accepted an appointment as Deputy US Marshal for the region. Three years later, he turned in his badge and left for California. He made a return visit to Grant County in 1892, supposedly the last time anyone ever saw him. At that point, the legendary and all-but-forgotten lawman vanished. Where he went from Grant County is unknown and when, how and where he died remains a mystery.

TWENTY-EIGHT

DEFYING
THE ODDS

WHEN THE SOUTHERN PACIFIC ARRIVED AT THE TRAIN STA-
TION IN TINY FAIRBANK, ARIZONA, A FEW MILES WEST OF
TOMBSTONE, TO OFFLOAD SOME CARGO ON THE NIGHT OF
FEBRUARY 15, 1900, SEVERAL GUNMEN MINGLED IN THE AWAITING
CROWD, PRETENDING TO BE DRUNK.

Former deputy sheriffs Bill Stiles and Burt Alvord planned to
rob the Wells Fargo express car that carried either the US Army
payroll for solders at Fort Huachuca, or a shipment of gold and
silver bullion. To help carry out the plan, the pair recruited Bob
Brown (or Burns), George and Louis Owens, "Brave Juan" Tom
Yoas, and "Three Fingered' Jack" Dunlop.

Jeff Milton, a former lawman and accomplished Manhunter,
had been working for the railroad as an express messenger. Aware
of Milton's gun skills, Stiles and Alvord decided to rob the train on

a night he wasn't working. When the express door opened, however, it was Jeff Milton who stepped out into the Thursday night moonlight. Milton had agreed to take a friend's place as a substitute messenger.

The situation unfolded fast. One of the gunmen in the crowd shouted at Milton to get his hands up. One of them shot at him. Milton's revolver was on the desk several feet away, his sawed-off shotgun inside the doorway. But he hesitated using it for fear of hitting an innocent bystander. The delay cost him. The next bullet shattered his left shoulder, sending him to the floor. In pain and losing blood, he crawled to the shotgun. He rolled to face the door just in time to see Three-Fingered Jack climbing into the railcar. Milton fired. Dunlap grasped his chest and dropped.

Yoas was close behind, but one of the buckshot pellets struck him in the leg or backside and he limped to his horse and galloped away. The gunmen fired again, but Milton somehow was able to slide the metal door closed amid ricocheting bullets. Struggling from loss of blood, Milton fashioned his own tourniquet. Growing weaker and in danger of passing out, he managed to get hold of the key to the express box and hurl it behind some luggage just before the outlaws gained entrance to the express car.

The gunmen found Milton sprawled on the floor in a pool of blood. Figuring he was dead, they searched his pockets, and the desk drawer, but couldn't locate the key. Frustrated and unable to find a way to open the express box, they had no choice but to leave. They took the injured Dunlap with them, but a posse found the gang member abandoned in the road, a few miles from Tombstone. He died within the week, but not before revealing the names of his outlaw associates, who were later captured and sent to prison.

Although Milton lost the use of his arm, and was considered permanently disabled, he continued his law enforcement career. Over the years, Milton had achieved an enviable record of public service. Before taking the job as shotgun messenger for Wells Fargo, he worked as a Texas Ranger, a deputy sheriff, police chief, deputy US marshal, and US customs border patrol agent. Four years after the shoot-out, he became an agent for the US Immigration Service under the Chinese Exclusion Act, assigned to stop the smuggling of Chinese aliens through Arizona and California, a job he held until 1932.

Born Jefferson Davis Milton in Marianna, Florida, in 1861, on the family plantation, he was the son of Confederate Governor John Milton, who committed suicide after the Civil War. At 16, Milton left for Texas where he lied about his age to make himself eligible to join the Texas Rangers. He died in Tucson on May 7, 1947, at age 86, his body cremated and his ashes spread across the Arizona desert where he spent so much of his life.

TWENTY-NINE

FACE-TO-FACE WITH A DEADLY GUNMAN

WHEN TEXAS RANGER JOHN B. ARMSTRONG ENTERED THE PAS-
SENGER COACH OF THE TRAIN AT PENSACOLA JUNCTION, ON
FRIDAY, AUG. 24, 1877, HE SWITCHED HIS CANE TO THE LEFT
HAND, DREW HIS COLT .45 WITH THE OTHER, AND AIMED IT AT THE
ESCAPED KILLER AND FOUR MEMBERS OF HIS GANG.

"Texas, by God!" outlaw John Wesley Hardin cried out, register-
ing surprise at seeing Armstrong.

One of the gang members grabbed his six-gun, and squeezed
off a shot at the lawman, but missed. Armstrong fired back, killing
him. Hardin tried to go for his gun, but it got tangled in his sus-
penders. Armstrong hurried down the aisle, slammed the long-bar-
reled revolver over Hardin's head, knocking him out, and disarmed
the other three. The Texas Ranger had been hunting Hardin for

three years in connection with his killing of Brown County Deputy Sheriff Charles Webb in May 1874.

The outlaw had been captured in Louisiana in September 1874 and returned to Texas, but escaped. Armstrong, recuperating from a gunshot wound that forced him to use a cane, made it his personal mission to track Hardin down and bring him to justice. Born in McMinnville, Tennessee, in January 1850, Armstrong kicked around Missouri and Arkansas for a time before moving to Austin, Texas, in 1871 where he joined the Travis Rifles. On May 20, 1875, he enlisted in the Texas Rangers, assigned to Captain Leander McNelley's Special Force. His career was rather brief, but he was responsible for important contributions to the agency.

After retiring, he was appointed a US Marshal. In 1882, he decided to step away from law enforcement and used $4,000 of the reward money for capturing Hardin to purchase 50,000 acres of cattle land in Willacy County, calling it the XIT Ranch, one of the largest at the time. The Armstrong Ranch helped pioneer new ranching techniques. It remains an active working ranch, today. Armstrong also put his muscle behind the campaign to bring railroads to South Texas. He joined a special Ranger division in the 1890s that to help the main organization deal with gunmen and cattle rustlers throughout the region.

He died May 1, 1913, and is one of thirty Rangers honored in the Texas Ranger Hall of Fame in Waco for giving their lives in the line of duty or for making significant contributions to the development of the agency.

THIRTY

PAT GARRETT'S HIGHS & LOWS

AT GARRETT, THE MAN WHO KILLED BILLY THE KID, KEPT HIS
EYES ON THE ROAD AS HE GUIDED THE BUCKBOARD ALONG
MAIL-SCOTT ROAD TOWARD LAS CRUCES, NEW MEXICO. HE
GREW TIRED OF LISTENING TO THE ARGUMENT UNDERWAY BETWEEN
HIS PASSENGER, CARL ADAMSON, AND THE MAN ON HORSEBACK,
JESSE WAYNE BRAZEL.

Adamson, and a partner, were interested in buying Garrett's
Bear Canyon Ranch. The once-famous lawman wanted to sell the
property to help alleviate growing financial obligations caused
by a series of bad investments. The potential sale, however, hit a
snag. Garrett had leased the ranch to Brazel, who gave the impression he was going to use the land to graze cattle. Brazel, he later
learned, began using the rangeland for a goat-raising venture.
Garrett seethed with anger at being duped. Goats, he knew, could

be destructive on vegetation and in other ways, as well. But all legal efforts to break the lease failed. Furthermore, Brazel said he would only agree to cancel the lease if the potential buyer bought the 1,800 goats along with the rest of the ranch.

About four miles from the ranch, situated in the San Andreas Mountains, Brazel rode up and joined Garrett and Adamson. Minutes later, he and Adamson engaged in a heated argument over the goats. Garrett hurled his own threat at Brazel, saying he intended to get the goats off his property in any way necessary. A mile or two later, Garrett stopped the buckboard so he and Adamson could relieve themselves. With their backs turned, a gunshot echoed through the gray and cloud covered Saturday morning of February 29, 1908.

The bullet slammed into the back of Garrett's head spinning him around. Another bullet caught him in the stomach as he fell backwards onto the hard-packed earth. Adamson turned quickly and saw Brazel holding a smoking revolver, which he gave to Adamson. The two men rode into Las Cruces where Brazel turned himself over to the law, claiming he had shot Garrett in self-defense.

When Garrett put a bullet in Billy the Kid in 1881, it pretty much assured his fame as a lawman and gunman. Despite dying so young, the Kid left a long shadow across the history of the American West. Arguments ranged far and wide on just how Garrett killed the Kid. Some say it was a cold-blooded ambush. Garrett claims the Kid was armed, but no weapons were ever found on him.

Garrett left his own imprint on the West, but one smudged by less-than-questionable decisions. Despite the mystery surrounding Billy the Kid's death, Garrett's star soared for a while. As sheriff of Lincoln County, New Mexico, he found himself in demand for a number of law enforcement posts, besieged with requests to hunt down outlaws in other parts of the state. After the shooting, Garrett experienced a series of highs and lows, even flirting with success as a farmer and businessman, until his investments turned sour. He became friends with President Theodore Roosevelt, who appointed Garrett as a customs agent in El Paso, Texas.

It was then that things began to unravel, and hard times came calling, mostly because of Garrett's own questionable behavior. The success he once enjoyed faded fast. He began drinking heavily and befriending individuals with unsavory reputations. Garrett's relationship with Roosevelt also went awry. The president ultimately viewed Garrett as a political liability, and refused to reappoint him.

After Garrett was killed, the jury went along with Brazel's argument of self-defense. The trial lasted one day. Deliberations took less than one-half hour. Brazel was found not guilty. No one really identified the triggerman. Garrett's friends contended he was the victim of a conspiracy, which was mostly likely true. Authorities had discovered several cigarette butts at the scene where Garrett was shot down, suggesting someone might have been waiting in ambush. The lawman made a lot of enemies during his years in law enforcement. But the case ended because of lack of proof.

THIRTY-ONE

A MAN NAMED OUTLAW

H IS NAME WAS OUTLAW, BUT HE WAS A LAWMAN. AND, HE KILLED THE ONE MAN HE COULD HAVE CALLED A FRIEND—THE *ONLY* TEXAS RANGER IN HISTORY TO KILL ANOTHER RANGER.

Baz (or *Bass*) Outlaw was born in Lee, Georgia, in 1854, exact date unknown. In fact, little information exists about his early years, except for his burning desire to become a Texas Ranger. But, he wouldn't pursue the dream until he was 30 when he left home and headed for Texas. Rumors persisted that Outlaw had fled Georgia, on the run from the law, because he murdered someone. Some people speculated Outlaw started the rumor himself, although he never to tried to distance himself from it.

Various historical accounts say Outlaw went to the nearest Ranger station when he arrived in Texas, submitted an application, got approved, and was assigned to Company E. Before long,

Outlaw gained considerable admiration among his fellow Rangers. He stood 5-foot-9, and weighed about 150 pounds, unassuming in physical appearance. Underestimating him, however, would be a mistake. His gun skills were unequalled. Not only was Outlaw pinpoint accurate with pistol or rifle, he was quick on the draw, a skill rare among his peers.

The new Ranger was on the fast track to success, thanks to a growing reputation as a proficient gunfighter, solid horseman, and capable tracker. Expectations were high. Gradually, however, a dark side began to emerge behind Outlaw's cold demeanor, a nasty disposition fueled by large quantities of demon rum.

"Bass had one weakness that—at last—proved to be stronger than all his virtues," said Texas Ranger Lon Oden. "Bass couldn't leave liquor alone, and when Bass was drunk, Bass was a maniac; none of us could handle him, none of us could reason with him, we just stayed with him until he sobered up."

Members of Company E complained so much, officials in 1887 transferred Outlaw to Company D, near Alpine, Texas. Three years later, they promoted him a couple of times and then put him in charge of the unit. Although he handled his new responsibilities well on the trail, he lacked competent administrative skills. Paperwork wasn't a strong suit. Furthermore, he failed to get control of his drinking, despite vowing several times to reform his ways. Ranger officials finally realized Outlaw's uncontrolled drinking and hair-trigger temper was too divisive, detrimental, and a danger to overall morale. On September 18, 1892, he was dishonorably discharged from the Rangers.

Outlaw stayed around Alpine long enough for US Marshal Dick Ware, an ex-Ranger, to hire him as a deputy US marshal in the early spring of 1894. On April 5, Outlaw joined Ware and two other deputies on a trip to El Paso for court hearings against several outlaws and cattle rustlers. Deputies, at the time, were paid fees based on how much work they contributed in preparing cases to be heard, including serving summonses and completing paperwork.

Since Deputy Bufe Cline handled most of the case preparation, Ware presented him the fees. Outlaw, who contributed little to the cases, exploded and argued the fees should have been split evenly. He and Marshal Ware exchanged strong words before Outlaw left the courthouse in an angry mood. He grew increasingly belligerent. While stumbling his way along Utah Street, he encountered Constable John Selman—the same John Selman who would shoot John Wesley Hardin in the back of the head a year later. When Outlaw boasted he was going to kill Marshal Ware, Selman tried to talk him into returning to his hotel room.

Outlaw refused and, instead, decided to visit his girlfriend who worked at Tillie Howard's, a local bordello. He went around to the back entrance, liquored up, and fired a shot, creating a disturbance. Tillie, the madam, ran out of her house blowing a police whistle to alert authorities of trouble. Among those responding was one-time fellow Texas Ranger, Private Joseph McKidrict, also in town for a court appearance, who had always admired and been friendly with Outlaw. He came around the corner and asked Bass why he had shot his gun. Outlaw answered by pointing his gun at McKidrict and firing, striking the private in the head and back, killing him on the spot.

Outlaw then swung his gun toward Selman and fired again, almost hitting the constable in the face. Selman returned fire, and the bullet hit Outlaw in the chest. The ex-Ranger staggered and, before falling, managed to snap off one more shot, wounding Selman in the leg. Outlaw collapsed, and was helped to a nearby saloon. The one-time Texas Ranger died four hours after the killing of a fellow Texas Ranger.

THIRTY-TWO

LARGE & IN CHARGE

T HE STAGE FROM TOMBSTONE TO BENSON, CROWDED WITH EIGHT PASSENGERS, MAINTAINED AN EASY PACE ALONG A RUGGED STRETCH OF ROADWAY SURROUNDED BY BARREN LAND.

Darkness approached as the sun continued its descent behind a distant line of mountains, casting long, misshapen shadows across the San Pedro River Valley. It was a Tuesday night, March 15, 1881. At the reins of the Kinnear & Company stagecoach was Eli "Bud" Philpot, one of the best-known stagecoach drivers around. Before traveling to Arizona, he had achieved an enviable reputation as a skilled handler for major stage lines in California. Sitting next to Philpot was Bob Paul, the shotgun messenger for Wells, Fargo & Co. Below his feet in the front boot, was a treasure box containing $26,000 in silver bullion, equivalent to about $620,000 in today's dollars.

About two hundred yards from Drew Station, just outside Contention City, the stage made its way up a steep incline. When a man stepped out of a grove of cottonwoods, gun in hand, Philpot pulled back hard on the reins. The gunman raised his hand into the air and order the stage to stop. Seconds later, several more road agents appeared, and two shots rang out in the darkness.

Paul ducked, but one of the bullets struck Philpot, who tumbled off the front of the coach, reins still in hand. Paul later said he thought the shot that killed Philpot had been meant for him. Paul lifted the shotgun and fired both barrels. Outlaw Bill Leonard, howled in pain when the bullet struck him in the groin. The commotion spooked the horses into a dead run. Paul grabbed his revolver and emptied its chambers until the stage was out of range of the bandits.

He got the team under control, coaxed the horses to stop, and leaped to the ground to check on the passengers. One of them, Peter Roerig, had been killed. Paul guided the stage into Benson, and telegraphed Wyatt Earp, who put together a posse to search for the outlaws. Paul later joined the same posse in an 18-day chase that failed to track down the outlaws.

Robert Paul, literally, traveled around the globe to get to Arizona. Born in Massachusetts on June 12, 1830, Paul hopped aboard a whaling ship at age twelve and traveled throughout the world. He arrived in San Francisco in 1849, at the height of the gold rush. Although he didn't make it as a prospector, Paul did find a profession that suited him: the law. He served a short time as a constable and as sheriff of California's Calaveras County, from 1859 to 1864.

An imposing figure at six-foot-six and 240 pounds, Paul went to work for Wells Fargo as a shotgun messenger. He did so well, the company transferred him to Arizona in 1877 to investigate a series of gold bullion robberies. He quickly became friends with Pima County Deputy Sheriff Wyatt Earp. Three years later, while working as US deputy marshal, he decided to run for Pima County Sheriff on the Republican ticket. Although it was believed he had the election well in hand over Democrat Charlie Shibell, the county Board of Supervisors certified Shibell as sheriff.

A week later, Paul accused Shibell and his supporters of massive voter fraud. While the courts were wrangling with the case, Paul rejoined Wells Fargo and rode shotgun for the stage that came under attack at Drews Station. The following month, April 1881, the Territorial Supreme Court awarded the election to Paul. But he left office in 1886 following another disputed election.

He served as Under Sheriff of Tucson until he died at home on March 26, 1901 at the age of 69. Bob Paul spent fifty years of his life in some form of law enforcement on two of the wildest frontiers in the American West—California and Arizona.

THIRTY-THREE

NO-NONSENSE MANHUNTER

THE SMALL POSSE OF DEPUTY US MARSHALS, LED BY HENRY "HECK" THOMAS, TRACKED THE AARON PURDY GANG TO A STILL ON THE SNAKE RIVER IN INDIAN TERRITORY ON JUNE 27, 1888.

Purdy and the others—wanted for moonshining, horse stealing, and train robbery—were cornered in a ravine, behind a barricade of brush and rocks, in Indian Territory. Thomas instructed deputies Burrell Cox, Hank Childers, and Jim Wallace, to stay out of sight while he gave the gang a chance to surrender. Approaching the ravine on horseback, he called out for Purdy to surrender. The answer was swift and deadly as the outlaws opened fire.

Two bullets struck Thomas, one in his right arm and the other in his left side, and toppled him from his horse. Apparently thinking Thomas was alone, Purdy and the others emerged from hiding to finish off the marshal. But, Cox and the other two deputies came out of hiding, shot and killed Purdy, and then arrested the others.

Thomas developed a reputation as one of the most effective lawmen in the Oklahoma Territory. Born January 6, 1850, in Oxford, Georgia, he was the youngest of 12 children. At age twelve, Thomas joined his father and uncle and headed off to fight in the Civil War on the battlefields of Virginia. Thomas served as a courier, while his father and uncle were commissioned officers in the 35th Georgia Infantry. In 1863, he contracted typhoid fever and was sent home to his family in Athens. Eventually, he joined the Atlanta police department. During his long career, Thomas worked as a policeman, express man, trail driver, and bounty hunter. His record of achievement earned him an appointment as a Deputy US Marshal for the Indian Territory, under US District Judge Isaac C. Parker. As a deputy marshal, he ended up making scores of arrests.

By 1889, Thomas and two other deputy US marshals—Chris Madsen and Bill Tilghman—teamed up to form what became known as the *Three Guardsmen*. Over a period of ten years, the trio arrested more than 300 outlaws, killing several of them. They were credited with bringing out the demise of the Wild Bunch, or Doolin Gang. In August 1896, Thomas led a posse that tracked Doolin down and killed him. They won high praise for helping bring law and order to the territory that would later become Oklahoma.

Despite his fame, his law enforcement responsibilities played havoc with Heck's family life. He and his wife Isabel had reared five children. But she had run out of patience with the rough life of the frontier and moved, with the children, back to Georgia. After the divorce, Thomas married Mattie Mowbray, although some accounts contend he was still lawfully married to Isabel. The couple had three children, although one died in infancy.

Thomas became the police chief of Lawton, Oklahoma, in 1902. But health problems were taking their toll and he lost the job seven years later. Heck Thomas died of Bright's Disease on August 14, 1912, in Comanche County. He was 62.

THIRTY-FOUR

A BROTHER
WHO HELD HIS OWN

UNFIRE FROM OUTSIDE THE COMIQUE VARIETY HALL IN DODGE
CITY, IN THE SUMMER OF 1878, PEPPERED THE INSIDE WALLS.
THE .45-CALIBER BULLETS NARROWLY MISSED THE TWO LAWMEN
INSIDE, SENDING THEM AND OTHERS, INCLUDING BAT MASTERSON,
TO THE FLOOR.

Seconds later Wyatt Earp and Jim Masterson scrambled to their
feet, ran outside, and exchanged shots with Texas cowboy George
Hoy who rode off. One of the shots struck Hoy and he tumbled to
the ground, a bullet wound in the arm. He died less than a month
later. No one knew for sure which lawman fired what ended up
being the fatal shot. Earp claimed he fired it. Although Masterson
didn't dispute it, many believed it was he who actually fired the
shot that brought down Hoyt because of his underplayed gun skills.

Masterson was the lesser-known brother of Bat Masterson and Ed Masterson, but it never seemed to bother him. Although James Masterson never achieved the fame that Bat enjoyed, it's believed he was involved in a higher number of shootouts than his well-known sibling. Another brother, Ed, had been killed in the line of duty a year earlier. (*Chapter 12, Showdown in Dodge City*). At the time of the Hoy shooting, James served as assistant marshal in Dodge City. He was promoted to marshal in 1879 after Charlie Bassett resigned. During the two years he spent in Dodge, Masterson made several hundred arrests. However, he lost the job in 1881 with a change of government, packed up, and left for Trinidad, Colorado, where he worked as a deputy.

James Masterson was the third of seven children, born in Iberville County, in Quebec Canada, on Sept. 18, 1855. In 1861, the family moved to the United States and spent time in New York state, and Illinois, before settling near Wichita, Kansas, in 1871. Several years later, he and his brothers left for the American western frontier where they made livings as buffalo hunters before relocating in Dodge.

From Trinidad, Masterson moved on to Colfax County, New Mexico Territory, where he served as under-sheriff, in 1885. He got involved in various high-profile cases as a lawman. Four years later in New Mexico, he took part in the Gray County (Kansas) County Seat War. He ended up in Guthrie, Oklahoma, and wore the badge of a deputy sheriff for Logan County. In 1893, he took an appointment of a US Marshal and found himself alongside other lawmen in the Ingalls, Oklahoma, shootout with the Doolin Gang.

Less than a year later, Jim Masterson was gone—dead from tuberculosis. At 39 years of age, he was buried in Wichita's Highland Cemetery. According to his obituary, "Jim Masterson was a man who never went back on a friend, and never forgot an obligation."

THIRTY-FIVE

THE
HANGING JUDGE

THE JOURNEY FROM MISSOURI TO ARKANSAS WAS LONG, TIR-
ING, AND GENERALLY UNCOMFORTABLE ABOARD THE STEAMBOAT
ELLA HUGHES, ITS PASSENGER CABINS NOTHING MORE THAN
WOODEN BUNKS WITH CURTAINS FOR PRIVACY.

Among its passengers was the newly appointed judge for the
Western District of Arkansas at Fort Smith. The man's family, who
stayed behind in Missouri, would join him sometime later. Judge
Isaac Parker wasted no time in establishing his presence. He arrived
at Fort Smith on May 4, 1875. Less than a week later, he appeared
on the bench for the first time. In the first term of the court, eight
men were found guilty of murder, subject to a federal law mandat-
ing the death sentence. A few months later on September 3, six
men were executed at the same time.

Isaac Charles Parker was born Oct. 15, 1838, just outside Barnesville, in Belmont County, Ohio. When he was seventeen, Parker decided to pursue a legal career, passed the bar exam in 1859, and moved to St. Joseph, Missouri. By 1861, he opened his own law firm, and earned a wealth of experience in the municipal court system. In April he was elected city attorney. In the fall of 1864, he served as a member of the Electoral College and cast a vote for Abraham Lincoln.

His interest in politics enabled Parker to win appointment as a judge for the Twelfth Missouri Circuit, and then was victorious in a race for Congress in 1870. With no chance for re-election, he parlayed his loyalty to the Republican Party into an appointment as judge of the Western District, in Fort Smith. Because of the heavy migration of settlers into the vast Indian Territory, crime spiraled. The first priority, however, was reform. Upon his arrival, he found the court disorganized and corrupt. His predecessor, William Story, had been impeached for bribery, and forced to resign.

Parker spent near twenty-two years as head of the US Court for the Western District of Arkansas. During his watch, he sentenced at least 160 people to death. Most US district judges spent their time on civil cases. Parker, on the other hand, dealt with thousands of criminal cases, many of which involved disputes and violence between Indians and non-Indians. His sentencing powers were carried out over a fourteen year period, a time when the condemned had no right of appeal. Parked appointed George Maledon as Lord High Executioner. (*Chapter 36, Hang 'em High*).

Seventy-nine were executed, forty-three were commuted to life in prison or lesser terms. Two won presidential pardon. Thirty-one filed appeals and were either acquitted or had their convictions overturned. Two were granted new trials and set free. One of the prisoners was shot and killed trying to escape. A couple of others died in jail while awaiting execution.

Although Parker has often been referred to as the *Hanging Judge*, the term didn't appear until 1920—nearly thirty years after he died.

> *"I have ever had the single aim of justice in view..." Parker wrote in 1896, "'Do equal and exact justice,' is my motto, and I have often said to the grand jury, 'Permit no innocent man to be punished, but let no guilty man escape."*

THIRTY-SIX

HANG 'EM HIGH

THE CROWD WAS QUIET, THE AIR STILL, AS THE MAN IN THE BLACK SUIT, A TWO-GUN RIG STRAPPED AROUND THE OUTSIDE OF HIS COAT, STEPPED ACROSS THE PLANKS OF THE GALLOWS, THE WOOD CREAKING BENEATH HIS BOOTS.

The executioner stopped, turned, and studied the condemned man's face, lathered with perspiration. The prisoner's eyes, drained of hope, reflected only the fear of what was about to take place. Judgment day had arrived.

George Maledon, a small quiet man with dark eyes, became known as the *Prince of Hangmen*. He carried out his responsibility with great pride and repetitive ritual. About a week before an execution, he spent time stretching the ropes by attaching them to a sack filled with mostly dirt to test the gallows trapdoor. Six times the trapdoor swung open, and six times the heavy bag plummeted into the darkness below. The sound echoed through the empty courtyard with a fury and finality easily heard by those awaiting execution.

Maledon procured rope made only of the finest hemp. And, he tied the knot in such a way that it would snap the neck of the condemned the instant he or she dropped through the opening. Maledon did everything possible to avoid the spectacle of someone strangling. On this particular day, the prisoner trembled as Maledon lowered the noose over his head and around the neck. Before tightening it, Maledon shook the hand of the convicted and whispered his goodbye with a few words of advice. "Once the rope is adjusted, don't move your head, and this will all go quickly," he counseled, pulling a black cap over the condemned man's face.

George Maledon, raised by immigrants in Detroit, Michigan, worked as a machinist by trade and an executioner by choice. He traveled to Fort Smith, Arkansas, in his late teens and joined the city police force. Maledon fought for the Union Army during the Civil War. After the war, he returned to Fort Smith and won appointment as US deputy marshal. When Fort Smith needed an executioner, he volunteered to take the job along with his regular activities as marshal.

In 1875, Isaac Parker was named federal judge of the Western District of Arkansas, headquartered at Fort Smith, one of the most corrupt areas of the country. It included the Indian Territory, known as a haven for killers, thieves, rustlers, and fugitives. Parker wasted no time in implementing a program to bring many of the criminals into custody. In his first few months on the job, his deputy marshals rounded up ninety-one defendants. Eight were sentenced to hang.

As chief executioner, he was paid $100 for each hanging. Once, he told an interviewer how he felt about his job.

"It certainly is not a very pleasant job, but I have become so accustomed to it that it now has no effect on me. I have got the business down fine, and know just how to prepare a noose and how to adjust one to make a complete and successful job.

"Of course I feel sorry for any man who is so unfortunate as to get himself hung, but at the same time think a larger share of my sympathy is due the other fellow—the one that has been murdered."

In 1895 Maledon's daughter, 18-year old Annie Maledon, was murdered by Frank Carver. Although he was convicted by Parker and sentenced to death, Carver managed to win a reprieve by way of an appeal to Washington. Maledon was so angry and disgusted by the decision he retired from his post as executioner and left Fort Smith. A few years later, he toured the nation, appearing at carnivals and fairs, standing inside a tent displaying some of the nooses he used, along with pieces of the gallows' beam, and photographs of some of the men he hanged.

THIRTY-SEVEN

AVENGING
RANGER

GRIEF OVERCAME TEXAS RANGER SCOTT COOLEY WHEN NEWS ARRIVED AT HIS RANGER CAMP, IN MAY OF 1875, THAT THE MAN WHO ADOPTED HIM HAD BEEN GUNNED DOWN BY A BRUTAL MOB NEAR MASON, TEXAS.

After crying over the loss of his mentor, Cooley wiped away the tears and vowed revenge. Cooley, born in Oklahoma, was orphaned in his early teens. After a cattle drive, rancher Tim Williamson took the teen to his home in Mason County. A few years later, Cooley joined the Texas Rangers.

Williamson, meanwhile, had the misfortune of getting caught in the middle of a blood feud called the *Hoodoo War*, or the Mason County War of 1875, a conflict triggered over the stealing and killing of cattle. Also at issue was cattle ownership between German settlers in the Mason County area and American-born men, living in neighboring counties. A few months earlier, the 33-year old Williamson, who also worked as a foreman for Carl Lehmberg, had been falsely arrested for stealing a calf. Lehmberg posted bond for his foreman who went back to work. On the morning of May 13, 1875, Deputy Sheriff John Wohrle rode out to tell Lehmberg and Williamson the bond had been revoked.

Lehmberg and Williamson, a popular cowboy, agreed to accompany Wohrle into town to post a new bond. The deputy disarmed Williamson and, at the same time, traded Williamson's young, fast horse for Wohrle's older mount. Ten miles later, a dozen masked men stopped the trio, and one of them shot Williamson's horse out from under him. Some accounts point to Deputy Wohrle (sometimes spelled Worley) as the shooter. On foot and without a weapon, Williamson never stood a chance and was gunned down by several members of the gang.

The armed mob worked for Sheriff John Clark, a man who was elected October 1873 by the German majority of Mason County. Not much was known about Clark. No one knew where he came from. And, when he left two years later, no one knew where he went. The nature of the Mason County War changed when Williamson was killed. Instead of a range war, it deteriorated into a violent, ethnic conflict. Cattlemen wanted vengeance and the one man who could deliver it was Scott Cooley. First, the former Ranger waited to see if the grand jury issued indictments in the Williamson killing. None were, and no one was arrested.

Cooley put together a list of the men he believed were responsible for Williamson's death. He also formed his own band of desperadoes, which included gunmen Johnny Ringo. Taking matters into his own hands, Cooley and his men rode to Wohrle's home where the deputy was working on a well with a helper. Cooley shot and killed the lawman without a second thought, firing five bullets into him. He then scalped the dead man so he could display it to the Germans, and then tossed the body down the well. Next on the list was cattleman Peter Brader, who was identified as the first man to shoot Williamson.

One-by-one, Cooley served as the avenging angel. A dramatic change came over Scott Cooley once he had killed the deputy. People say he became withdrawn, wore his hat down low to hide his eyes, and never paid much paid attention to anyone. One account says Cooley declined to shake hands with anyone for fear his gun hand wouldn't be available for a second or two. The killings continued, back and forth, over the next several months.

In December 1875, authorities arrested Cooley and Ringo and jailed them in Lampasas County, Texas. Friends helped the two of them break out. During the escape, a posse managed to corner Cooley at the Llanno River, but he got away and hid out with friends in Blanco County. In the meanwhile, Johnny Ringo was recaptured and stood trial, and was acquitted. Cooley disappeared. Some say he might have died from wounds received while fleeing from the posse. Others contend he died from what was believed to be brain fever. He was 31.

THIRTY-EIGHT

BATTLE OF WALKER'S CREEK

RIEF GLINTS OF SUNLIGHT FLICKERED THROUGH THE CANOPY OF SWAYING TREE BRANCHES AS FOURTEEN RIDERS, ALL TEXAS RANGERS, GUIDED THEIR HORSES ALONG THE TRAIL BORDERING THE MEANDERING PEDERNALES RIVER, ITS WATER TINTED GREEN FROM THE REFLECTION OF LARGE CYPRESS TREES ALONG THE BANK.

Captain John Coffee Hays and his men were on the hunt for a war party of Penateka Comanche under the command of Chief Yellow Wolf who conducted several raids throughout Bexar County, in south-central Texas. The Rangers, who left their headquarters in San Antonio around June 1, 1844, scouted the hills north and west but couldn't locate the raiding party. Nine days later, the patrol made camp at Walker's Creek, at the Pinta Trail Crossing of the Guadalupe River.

Sometime the next day, a highly emotional scout warned Hays that "about a thousand Indians" were trailing the Rangers. After a second look, it was estimated there were between forty and seventy-five warriors. When the approaching Comanche arrived at Walker's Creek, they spread out, concealing themselves in brush and timber along a hill. A few, however, revealed themselves in an effort to taunt the Rangers into a frontal assault.

"Jack" Hays had made a thorough study of the Comanche ways. He admired their fighting style so much, he copied their tactics, and also trained his men to ride and shoot as well as the Comanche. Despite all the preparation, Hays knew the Rangers lacked sufficient firepower to take the fight to the Comanche. Rangers, until the Battle of Walker's Creek, normally carried single-shot rifles. The Comanche relied on lethal longbow archers and, in the time it took Rangers to reload the single-shot rifles between shots, the Indians could unleash a downpour of arrows. But, this time, the Comanche were in for a surprise.

Back in Connecticut, a man by the name of Samuel Colt had developed and patented a revolving pistol, but he didn't sell many of them. In fact, the military avoided them, perhaps because it lacked a trigger guard, and featured a folding trigger. Even with these drawbacks, Hays still believed in the new Colt. Texas President Mirabeau Lamar ordered a shipment for the Texas Navy, but there's no documentation the navy ever used the new weapons. Somehow, Hayes convinced Lamar to provide enough of the five-shot Colt Paterson to arm his Texas Rangers.

At Walker Creek, Hays led his men around a ravine and attacked the enemy from behind. The Comanche, however, managed to regroup and launched a counter-attack from two sides. Rangers quickly formed a circle with their horses and began firing with their new Colt repeating revolvers. Since the Rangers didn't carry extra pre-loaded cylinders, or extra weapons, they had to make every shot count. The Comanche were stunned by the firepower, confused as to why the Rangers weren't reloading after every shot. The Rangers kept shooting until their Colt cylinders were empty.

As more Comanche died, a perplexed Yellow Wolf signaled his war party to retreat. When they did, Hays ordered his men to give chase and keep firing until they ran out of ammo. Hays knew that, in order to survive a fight, it was important to kill the tribal leader. When a chief was killed, the Comanche would break off their attack and flee. As the gunsmoke around Walker's Creek began to dissipate, Hays asked if any of his men had any bullets left. Roger Gillespie stepped forward and told Hays he had one round left. He ordered Gillespie to dismount and shoot Yellow Wolf. When the Ranger fired the fatal shot, the rest of the Comanche raiding party retreated, but Hays decided not to give chase.

The Rangers suffered one casualty, but the Comanche lost at least twenty warriors. Among the wounded was Samuel Walker. He would eventually collaborate with Samuel Colt to create the Walker Colt, a gun that revolutionized warfare and played a key role in the history of the West. Thanks to Jack Hays, the Battle at Walker's Creek signaled a turning point in Indian warfare because it marked the first time that repeating firearms were effective in close combat with the Comanche.

THIRTY-NINE

THE BAD, THE GOOD, & THE DEAD

J OHN KING FISHER REIGNED AS ONE OF THE MOST FEARED OUTLAWS IN SOUTH TEXAS BUT OVER THE YEARS TRANSI- TIONED INTO A RESPECTED RANCHER AND AN EFFECTIVE AND POPULAR LAWMAN.

Fisher started out on the wrong side of the law early in life. By age sixteen, he was accused of horse stealing, arrested for house-breaking, and sentenced to a two-year term in the Texas state penitentiary. Fisher, however, was pardoned February 1871 after serving just four months because of his age and good behavior. After leaving prison, Fisher traveled to Dimmit County, where he established his own ranch on the Pendencia Creek, situated near Eagle Pass on the border of Mexico. The ranch was located along the Nueces Strip in south Texas, where cattle rustlers operated unchecked.

Fisher's spread soon became a haven for drifters and outlaws to support his growing power as a leader of the Strip, controlling about five thousand square miles from Castroville to the Rio Grande River. Accounts say he sometimes joined Mexican rustlers and managed to carve out about a hundred head of stolen cattle for himself. Rumors also persisted that Fisher once traded cattle with the eventual president of Mexico, Porfirio Diaz. An imposing figure, Fisher wore a black Mexican jacket embroidered in gold, a crimson sash wrapped around his waist, and an ornamental sombrero. His two holsters carried two silver-plated, ivory-handled revolvers.

Historians say Fisher had a quick temper and achieved a reputation as a skilled gunfighter. He was also intimidating. As a symbol of his power and control, Fisher nailed a painted sign to a tree along the road leading to his ranch. It warned: "This is King Fisher's road. Take the other." His questionable activities brought him into direct confrontation with the Texas Rangers, who arrested him several times and charged him with murder and stealing cattle and horses. Fisher always found a way to avoid conviction.

Somewhere along the way, Fisher got fed up bumping heads with the law. He married Sarah Vivian in April 1876 and settled down on a ranch near Eagle Pass. The couple eventually had four daughters. A few years later, he ended up enforcing the law instead of breaking it when he was appointed deputy sheriff of Uvalde County. Two years later, he became sheriff.

He was so effective and popular that he decided to run for re-election in 1884. In March of the same year, he traveled to Austin, hooked up with his friend Ben Thompson, a well-known gunfighter, and the two decided to board a train to San Antonio. The city, however, wasn't a safe place for Thompson because of a feud between him and the owners of the Vaudeville Variety Theater.

After the two men took in a play that night at the Turner Hall Opera House, they made their way to the theater. It was 10:30. Later in the evening, Thompson demanded to see Joe Foster, one of the owners. Thompson and Fisher were directed upstairs to the balcony where an argument ensued. The two men had unknowingly been lured into an ambush. Gunmen pumped several shots into Thompson's head. Fisher's body revealed thirteen bullets. Accounts of the ambush, to this day, differ in detail. Although demands emerged for a grand jury investigation, neither the San Antonio police nor prosecutor took action.

John King Fisher, who often lived by the gun, died by the gun at age 30. He was buried on his ranch in his familiar colorful attire. His body was later moved to the Pioneer Cemetery in Uvalde, Texas.

FORTY

CHRISTMAS EVE AMBUSH

O N A GREY AND CLOUDY CHRISTMAS EVE AFTERNOON IN 1886, SAM SIXKILLER FELT A BIT UNDER THE WEATHER, SO HE RODE INTO MUSKOGEE, OKLAHOMA, TO PICK UP SOME MEDICINE.

Unarmed and off-duty, the deputy marshal swung down from the saddle, walked into a store and retrieved his medication, and then left. As he stepped onto the walkway, two men emerged from the shadows to confront him. The pair, according to historians, held a grudge against Sixkiller because of a previous run-in. Alf Cunningham stood holding a shotgun, and Dick Vann, his brother-in-law, leveled a pistol. The quick-acting Sixkiller knocked the shotgun to the side, but Vann fired squeezed off several shots, and Sixkiller collapsed, dead from the bullet wound.

During the Civil War, Sam Sixkiller served on *both* sides—first as a private in the 1st Cherokee Cavalry of the Confederacy. Later, he joined the Union Army so he could serve under his father, 1st Lt. Redbird Sixkiller. The name *Sixkiller,* historians contend, originated with Sam's great grandfather. In a fight between the Cherokees and the Creeks, according to legend, the ancestor killed six of the enemy before being killed himself. From that point on, the name *Sixkiller* passed from father to son and, finally, to Sam.

Sam Sixkiller was born in 1842 in the Going Snake district of the Cherokee Nation, in Indian Territory, now Adair County, Oklahoma. After the war, he held several law enforcement posts, including the high sheriff of the Cherokee Nation, and warden of the National Penitentiary in 1875. Five years later, Sixkiller became the first captain of the Indian Police. Headquartered at Muskogee, Indian Territory, he provided law enforcement services for the lands of all five tribes. Under his command were a hundred men, with another 300 in reserve.

After he was appointed US Deputy Marshal, he chased outlaws down throughout Indian Territory, as well as Arkansas, Kansas, Missouri, and Texas. As special agent for the Missouri-Pacific Railroad, Sixkiller's duties included policing the streets of Muskogee, considered one of the most dangerous towns in the West. During the frontier era, more lawmen lost their lives in a fifty-mile radius of Muskogee than anywhere west of the Mississippi River.

Sixkiller and the forty men under his command spent several years going up against killers, train robbers, cattle rustlers, and bootleggers. Among them: notorious outlaw Dick Glass. In 1885, Sixkiller and his men waited in ambush for Glass at Colbert's Landing on the Red River, in the Chickasaw Nation. Glass, and his gang, had ridden into Dennison, Texas, to pick up a load of whiskey. When they neared Colbert's Landing, Sixkiller ordered them to surrender, but guns from both sides began blazing. When the smoke settled, Glass was among those killed, allegedly by Sixkiller. Several escaped, but were later apprehended.

After Sam Sixkiller was ambushed, the turnout for his Sunday morning funeral was so large the church couldn't accommodate the gathering of family friends, and fellow lawmen, who traveled from every part of the Territory. Accounts also say the procession, after the church service, ranked as one of the largest ever assembled in that part of the country.

A $1,500 reward was offered for the arrest of the two men who gunned down Sixkiller. Despite an intensive manhunt, the pair was never caught.

FORTY-ONE

INVITATION TO
A HANGING

A HANGING ISN'T AN APPROPRIATE EVENT TO COAX A SMILE FROM OTHERS, BUT AN ARIZONA LAWMAN THOUGHT OTHERWISE AND HIS CREATIVE FREEDOM WAS MET WITH PURE OUTRAGE.

Navajo County Sheriff Frank Wattron thought it might be clever to issue a specially-worded invitation to the 1899 hanging of back-shooter George Smiley. His attempt at literary license, however, provoked responses of anger and resentment as high up as the White House. President William McKinley issued a letter of condemnation to the territorial governor, objecting to Wattron's literary license:

"You are cordially invited to attend the hanging of one GEORGE SMILEY, Murderer. His soul will be swung into eternity on Dec. 8, 1899, at 2 o'clock p.m., sharp. Latest methods in the art of scientific

strangulation will be employed, and everything possible will be done to make the proceedings cheerful and the execution a success."

Governor Nathan Oakes Murphy issued a proclamation delaying the hanging and reprimanding the sheriff:

"The sheriff of Navajo County...has seen fit to publicly advertise and issue cards of invitation...in unseemly and flippant language, and in terms which have brought reproach upon the good name of this territory...."

Sheriff Wattron got in the last word, however, when he laced his invitation for the rescheduled hanging with an even deeper sarcastic tone than the first:

"With feelings of profound sorrow and regret, I hereby invite you to attend and witness the private, decent and humane execution of a human being; name, George Smiley; crime, murder.

The said George Smiley will be executed on Jan. 8, 1900, at 2 o'clock p.m. You are expected to deport yourself in a respectful manner, and any 'flippant' or 'unseemly' language or conduct on your part will not be allowed.

Conduct, on anyone's part, bordering on ribaldry and tending to mar the solemnity of the occasion will not be tolerated."

This time, Smiley went to the gallows, as scheduled.

Hangings were a common occurrence in the Old West, and most of them drew a crowd. Local law officers often sent actual printed invitations to attend the lynching. At times, the invitations were quite formal and printed on cards with gilt-edges.

It's not known how many hangings *Sheriff John Hicks Adams* planned to stage in a month's time. But the invitations he issued were pre-printed to read *San José, March___ 1875.* In this particular case, Adams inked in the number 16 for the day of the execution. At the bottom right of the invitation were the words *Not Transferable,* which sounds rather peculiar. Usually, a phrase like this appears on passenger tickets, or on licensed products. You wouldn't think to find in on an invitation to hang someone.

Hangings served as a source of popular public entertainment back in the 19th century—invitation or no invitation.

FORTY-TWO

BOTH SIDES OF THE LAW

OMPLICATED AND INCONSISTENT MIGHT BE THE BEST WAY
TO DESCRIBE SHERMAN MCMASTERS, WHO ONCE RODE THE
AMERICAN FRONTIER WITH SOME OF THE MOST RECOGNIZABLE
NAMES IN HISTORY.

McMasters, born 1853 into a wealthy Illinois family, was well educated but restless. He made his way West in his late teens or twenties and wasted no time in making a name for himself—first as a gunman, a Texas Ranger, and then as a lawman. McMasters traveled to Dodge City, Kansas, where he became friends with Wyatt Earp and Doc Holliday. He is, perhaps, best known for serving as a member of the posse assembled by Wyatt Earp for his so-called Vendetta Ride. Despite his inclination to side with the law, a story once surfaced that he killed a man over a gambling dispute in a saloon, but the incident was ruled self-defense.

Between 1878 and 1879, McMasters joined the Texas Rangers in El Paso County, where he chased horse thieves, tracked renegade Indians, and served as a scout for the 9th Cavalry. During the year he spent with the Texas Rangers, he met outlaw "Curly Bill" Brocius and had him in custody for about five months. A friendship was formed. Some accounts contend McMasters helped Brocius escape from jail. A short time later, after McMasters left the Rangers, he joined up with Curly Bill and two other men.

McMasters then made his way to Las Vegas, New Mexico, where he teamed up with Hoodoo Brown who ran the Dodge City Gang. McMasters, however, never stayed in one place long. His turned up next in Tombstone, Arizona, where he renewed his friendship with Brocius, Johnny Barnes, and Pony Diel—who happened to be friendly with the outlaw Clanton faction, called the Cowboys.

Despite his association with the Cowboys, McMasters remained on friendly terms with the Earp Brothers, who were now in Tombstone and at odds with the Clantons. Following the infamous shootout at the OK Corral, on Oct. 26, 1881, the Earps became targets for retribution. Morgan Earp was killed the following March. In another assassination attempt, Virgil Earp was seriously wounded when he took several bullets for his role in the now-famous gunfight. Although Wyatt Earp knew McMasters has been friendly with the Clanton group, he invited him to join the federally sanctioned posse that left on a mission to hunt down the Clanton desperados. McMasters' inside knowledge of the Clanton element proved valuable.

McMasters also proved helpful in other areas. He spoke fluent Spanish. His skill with a gun was well known. In fact, Thomas Masterson—Bat Masterson's brother—said McMasters was the fastest man on the draw he had ever seen. Some believe McMasters served as an undercover operative for Earp, and for Wells Fargo, too, but no proof existed. The Vendetta Ride didn't meet Wyatt

Earp's expectations because the Clanton brothers had already backtracked to Tombstone and turned themselves in.

On Jan. 30th, 1882, a deputy sheriff arrived at the Earp camp to serve a warrant on McMaster. He was accused of taking a couple of horses from a mine the previous fall. When the posse rode back to Tombstone, Earp bailed McMasters out of jail. Soon afterwards, McMaster disappeared—not only from Tombstone, but also from the pages of history.

Several stories followed. One report had him killed in a shoot-out with the Cowboy faction in 1884, supposedly after branding him a double-crosser. Earp, on the other hand, maintained McMasters died while serving as a soldier in the Spanish American War. But there is no evidence of either conclusion. His own siblings, however, said McMasters died in Colorado in 1892.

FORTY-THREE

FORMER SLAVE WORE A BADGE

A T SIX-FEET, TWO-INCHES, AND ABOUT 200 POUNDS, BROAD-SHOULDERED BASS REEVES FEARED NO ONE. AND, IF HIS PHYSICAL STATURE WASN'T ENOUGH OF A DETERRENT, THE FIRST BLACK AMERICAN TO RECEIVE A COMMISSION AS US DEPUTY MARSHAL WEST OF THE MISSISSIPPI RIVER WAS A DEADLY SHOT, WITH EITHER HAND.

"If Reeves were fictional, he would be a combination of Sherlock Holmes, Superman, and the Lone Ranger," said historian Art Burton.

Reeves, born a slave in Arkansas in 1838, found himself a free man 25 years later when President Lincoln issued the Emancipation Proclamation. He became skillful with firearms at an early age, and was considered a marksman with sidearms as well as long guns. During the late 1860s, Bass worked his own farm near Van Buren,

Arkansas. Every now and then he served as a guide and tracker in Indian Territory for deputy marshals. He carried two Colt pistols, holstered butt-forward.

After Judge Isaac Parker won an appointment to preside over the Western District Court of Arkansas, in 1875, he swore in a chief marshal and 200 deputy marshals to pursue criminals throughout 74,000 square miles of Indian Territory. When Parker learned that Bass Reeves could speak Indian language and was on friendly terms with various tribes, he offered him an appointment as US Deputy Marshal. Reeves agreed. It marked the beginning of a 32-year career as a lawman.

Reeves had no formal education and, according to various historical accounts, he could neither read nor write. But his memory was near flawless. Someone would read the warrants aloud, enabling Reeves to memorize the contents, which he would recite when necessary while carrying out his duties. He was also considered a master at disguises and aliases, often using them to make arrests. Reeves presented himself as a farmer, cowboy, gunman, and even an outlaw, at various times. During his career, Reeves arrested 3,000 felons and killed 14 men. But he never took a bullet himself.

Reeves carried out his duties, no matter how distasteful, including the arrest of his own son, Bennie, for killing his wife in a rage of jealousy. None of the other marshals wanted the assignment of tracking the young man down, so Reeves took the task himself. Two weeks later, he brought in his son who was eventually convicted and sent to Leavenworth.

In 1907, when Oklahoma, achieved statehood, Reeves retired from the federal marshal service. Although he was 67, Reeves took a job as city policeman in Muskogee, Oklahoma and worked for about two years. It was said that no crime occurred on his beat.

FORTY-FOUR

LAST OF THE OLD TIME SHERIFFS

O N THE MORNING OF JULY 4, 1888, GUNSHOTS RANG OUT IN THE STREETS OF FARMER CITY, KANSAS. A MAN BY THE NAME OF ED PRATHER AND A FRIEND DECIDED TO GET AN EARLY START ON CELEBRATING THE INDEPENDENCE DAY.

The disturbance went on for so long that Deputy Sheriff William Tilghman flagged down the pair and asked them to act more civil. Tilghman, celebrating his birthday, had been friends with Prather and reportedly helped him a number of times. But Prather took offense at Tilghman's request. So he and his friend moved the celebrating to neighboring Leoti.

When the two men returned later in the day, Prather continued his drinking, and the situation turned ugly. According to a local newspaper, he broke down a few doors demanding to be waited on and, at the same time, voiced insults and threats against Tilghman.

Prather apparently had a split personality. When sober, he was kind and generous. But, when he drank, he turned bitter and dangerous. He was also considered an expert with a .45. At about 7 p.m., Tilghman went to see Prather. The conversation grew heated and Prather reached for his gun. Tilghman warned him to take his hand off the weapon, but Prather refused. Seconds later, the sheriff fired twice and Prather fell dead.

Bill Tilghman, born at Fort Dodge, Iowa, July 4, 1856, led a colorful life. He served as a buffalo hunter, peace officer, a movie producer, and a state senator. Early in his career, Tilghman rode with the Earps, served as a deputy sheriff in Dodge City, Kansas, did battle with the Dalton gang and the Wild Bunch, and helped track down the Doolin gang. He devoted 51 years of his life to law enforcement, and was considered the last of the old-time sheriffs. Lawman and gunfighter Bat Masterson considered Tilghman "the greatest of us all." Tilghman wasn't particularly fast with a gun, but he was pinpoint accurate, and known for his courage.

About a year after shooting Prather, Tilghman moved to Oklahoma during the land rush of April 1889, and called Guthrie home. Appointed a deputy US Marshal, Tilghman held the job continuously for 19 years. In 1900, he won election as sheriff of Lincoln County, Oklahoma, got interested in politics, and was elected to the Oklahoma State Senate. He resigned the Senate in 1911 to return to law enforcement as the chief of police of Oklahoma City.

When he retired, he didn't like the way Hollywood glamorized the outlaws of the Old West, so he produced a movie in an effort to depict the reality of the frontier. It didn't do well. Theaters refused to show it because it lacked any big-name actors. Hollywood advised Tilghman to hired Tom Mix for the film, but the old lawman rejected the idea.

In 1924, some businessmen from the booming oil town of Cromwell, Oklahoma, contacted Tilghman, hoping to persuade him to accept the position of town sheriff. Cromwell was caught in the grip a rampant crime—bootlegging, gambling, and prostitution, and other illegal activities that were succeeding under the protection of a corrupt federal Prohibition agent named Wiley Lynn. Tilghman followed through on his promises to help bring things under control.

He closed down gambling houses, made a number of arrests, and ran the prostitutes out of town. The sheriff and Lynn tangled one night when Tilghman was enjoying dinner with friends at Ma Murphy's restaurant. In the confrontation, Lynn pulled out a .22 caliber pistol and shot Tilghman in the stomach. The lawman died there, surrounded by family and friends.

In 1925, Lynn was tried but acquitted of killing Tilghman. He was dismissed from his federal job. Seven years later, he was shot and killed by an agent for the Oklahoma Bureau of Investigation.

FORTY-FIVE

SHOOTOUT
AT THE OUTHOUSE

THE STREETS OF WICHITA, KANSAS, WERE DARK IN THE EARLY
MORNING OF FEBRUARY 28TH, 1871, WHEN DEPUTY US MARSHAL
JACK BRIDGES AND A DETACHMENT OF SOLDIERS FROM FORT
HARKER APPROACHED THE HARRIS HOUSE HOTEL.

Bridges carried an arrest warrant for "Handsome Jack" John
Ledford, who owned the hotel. Ledford had been implicated in the
robbery of a government wagon train during which several teamsters were killed. During the early days of Wichita, Kansas, Jack
Ledford and his Star-Bar-Half-Moon gang ruled the Arkansas River
Valley, raiding and robbing stage stagecoaches, counterfeiting, and
stealing horses. Authorities posted a $2,000 reward for bringing
Ledford to justice, dead or alive. An expert with a pistol, Ledford
could fire with either hand, and with deadly precision. At the end

of his two-year reign of crime, Ledford decided to put his outlaw days behind him. He got married, and went into the hotel business.

Marshal Bridges and Ledford had a history. A few months before, Ledford had pistol-whipped the marshal during an argument. Bridges wanted revenge and, according to newspaper accounts, vowed to shoot Ledford some day. When Bridges and the military detachment reached the hotel, an unidentified citizen told Bridges he spotted Ledford leaving the hotel and sneaking into an outhouse behind a nearby saloon. Bridges and his men surrounded the privy. The marshal barked an order to surrender, but Ledford ignored it.

Minutes later, the one-time outlaw swung the door open, and stepped out with guns blazing. One of his bullets ripped through Bridges' arm. In the return fire, the soldiers hit Ledford four times. He was carried to his home and attended to by a doctor but died less than an hour later.

Bridges, who had spent 15 years as a lawman, returned to his home in Maine to recuperate. He resumed his law enforcement career, first in Colorado, and then returned to Kansas where he served as city marshal of Dodge City. But a cloud of sorts had followed the lawman for the rest of his career. Newspaper reports had brought his character into question after the Ledford incident, suggesting that he never had legal grounds to arrest the outlaw. Bridges, however, continued to serve until his death in 1915.

FORTY-SIX

A WAY WITH GUNS & WORDS

WILLIAM BARCLAY MASTERSON STANDS AS ONE OF THE MORE MEMORABLE AND FASCINATING FIGURES IN HISTORY, BUT NOT ONLY FOR HIS IMAGE AS A FEARLESS WESTERN GUNFIGHTER, GAMBLER, AND LAWMAN.

Bat Masterson, as he was known, spent the last twenty years of his life carving a reputation as a newspaper columnist, and boxing authority, in New York City. The columns—*Masterson's Views on Timely Topics*—appeared in the *New York Morning Telegraph* three times a week. They covered a broad range of topics, including boxing and other sports, along with politics, crime, and society in general. Most readers considered him outspoken, and highly opinionated.

Born in Canada in 1853, Masterson traveled to Kansas and worked as a buffalo hunter and army scout in the Plains Indian

Wars. Eventually, he made his way to Dodge City where he and longtime friend Wyatt Earp served as law officers. In November 1877, Masterson waged a successful campaign for sheriff of Ford County, Kansas. He was twenty-two. When he lost a bid for re-election a couple of years later, Masterson took to the trail, roaming several legendary towns of the Old West making a living as a gambler. He also spent a year as a marshal in Trinidad, Colorado. During a visit to Tombstone, Arizona, he renewed his friendship with Deputy US Marshal Earp. Masterson, however, left prior to the infamous *Gunfight at the OK Corral,* although he later wrote about the confrontation.

Masterson's transition from frontier lawman and gunfighter to journalist appeared to have started while in Dodge. He published a one-edition-only political newspaper, *The Vox Populi,* in November 1885. Six years later, he moved to Denver, married an actress, and began writing a weekly sports column for *George's Weekly,* a local newspaper. While in Denver, he opened the Olympic Athletic Club to promote boxing.

When he moved to New York City in 1902, Masterson got arrested for running a crooked Faro game and carrying a concealed weapon. The charges were dropped, but he paid a ten-dollar fine on the concealed weapon charge. Masterson still flirted with a career in law and order while in New York, despite his interest in sports writing. In 1905, President Teddy Roosevelt appointed him US Marshal of the southern district of New York state. Two years later, however, he resigned, and went to work at the *Telegraph* as sports editor. It didn't take long to establish his presence. The former lawman died Oct. 25, 1921, at the age of 67, while working at his desk writing what would become the final column for the *New York Morning Telegraph.*

As with any character like Bat Masterson, stories enhance the legend. Some accounts say he found himself often amused and irritated by his reputation as a gunman. Once, a young man reportedly asked the former lawman for one of his guns, as a souvenir. The story goes that Masterson bought a pistol from a pawnshop, and carved 22 notches into the handle. The kid was duly impressed and asked Bat if he had really killed that many men.

"I didn't tell him yes and I didn't tell him no," said Masterson.

Different versions of this story remain in circulation. Masterson apparently displayed enviable accuracy with a six-shooter and often entertained others with "fancy hip shooting" demonstrations. He supposedly bought old guns at pawnshops, carved notches in to the handles, and sold them at inflated prices, suggesting the guns he sold were the ones he actually used during his career as a lawman.

FORTY-SEVEN

SHOWDOWN AT A MOUNTAIN STRONGHOLD

A GLIMMER OF SUNLIGHT SETTLED ACROSS THE HORIZON IN THE EARLY MORNING OF NOVEMBER 2, 1892, WHEN A SIXTEEN-MAN POSSE, MOVED INTO POSITION TO SURROUND A MOUNTAIN FORTRESS IN THE GOING SNAKE DISTRICT, A REMOTE AREA OF THE CHEROKEE NATION.

Heading up the posse was Deputy US Marshals Paden Tolbert and G.S. "Cap" White. Inside the double-walled log fortress was Ned Christie, a Cherokee statesmen accused of killing Deputy US Marshal Daniel Maples on May 4, 1887. Christie spent five years on the run, successfully evading capture. Twice before, posses attempted to flush him out of his wooden fortress, but twice they failed. This time, lawmen came well-armed with rifles, revolvers, small-arms ammunition, and dynamite. But Tolbert thought something more might be needed. He traveled 250 miles to Fort Scott, Kansas, to retrieve a cannon that fired three-pound shells.

When he returned, the posse spent the day firing over two thousand rounds of ammunition along with several shells from the cannon. Tolbert gets the credit for history's only use of a cannon against civilians by law enforcement. The withering firepower had little effect on Christie's mountain stronghold. At nightfall, under Tolbert's direction, the posse built a portable barricade from which to launch an attack. Using the barricade to protect themselves from Christie, who was firing from the second floor of the structure, they succeeded by blasting a hole in the walls with dynamite. The tactic forced Christie out into the open. When he tried to flee, the lawmen gunned him down.

In 1918, Christie was cleared of shooting Deputy Maples when a Cherokee freedman named Dick Humphrey came forward. He told a newspaper reporter that he witnessed Maples's murder and that Christie was not the assailant. Humphrey said he regretted not coming forward earlier, but couldn't speak up earlier for fear of retaliation. Some historians suggest that Christie may have been the victim of a conspiracy because of his opposition to railroad development in Indian Territory.

Tolbert became a US Deputy Marshal when he was 22, described by one of his peers as "one of the bravest men" to ever wear a Deputy US Marshal badge. He and his partner "Bud" Ledbetter succeeded in arresting several hard-core outlaws during their careers, including the Jennings Gang in 1897. Tolbert and Ledbetter also prevented an 1894 train robbery at Blackstone Switch, which ended in the arrest of Nathaniel "Texas Jack" and his outlaw gang.

He served with other legendary deputy marshals appointed by Judge Isaac Parker, including Heck Thomas and Bill Tilghman. Tolbert died April 28, 1904, of complications of lung congestion. He was 34.

FORTY-EIGHT

THE ROAD-TO-RUIN SALOON

Sheriff George Adolphus Scarborough sat in a saloon in Haskell, Texas, glanced up, and saw an outlaw by the name of A.J. Williams walk in—a man he had been pursuing for over three years.

Williams stood five-eight with coal black hair and cold gray eyes and led a gang cattle rustlers operating in the area. Scarborough and Williams had crossed paths in the past. Once Scarborough tracked him and a couple gang members to a ranch in Lincoln County, New Mexico Territory, but Williams escaped. The lawman returned a second time, captured him again, and returned him to Jones County, Texas, where Williams staged a breakout. Although he was captured, the gang leader eventually made bail and skipped town.

When Williams walked into "Whiskey, The Road to Ruin Saloon" on Saturday, October 15, 1887, Scarborough sat at a table writing a letter to his wife. His brother Will sat across from him. Although Scarborough sat with his back to the door, he faced a mirror where he had a clear few of the doorway. A witness said Williams drew his gun, but Scarborough spun around, gun in hand, and killed the outlaw with one shot. Scarborough and his brother were arrested and charged with murder. The jury took less than five minutes to return a verdict of not guilty.

He lost a bid for another term as sheriff in 1888 and moved to Deming, New Mexico, where he worked as a hired gun for the Grant County Cattlemen's Association. Five years later, he accepted an appointment as a deputy US marshal for the Western District of Texas.

Scarborough had little formal knowledge of law enforcement and relied mostly on courage and commonsense to make it from one day to the next. During his career, he built a reputation as tenacious manhunter who had no quit in him. Once, he arrested a suspect in a murder case committed twenty-eight years earlier. According to Robert K. DeArment, in his book, *George Scarborough: The Life and Death of a Lawman on the Closing Frontier*, the frontier peace officer most always left a lasting impression on others. Most remembered him as a big man with black hair and long, flowing moustache. In reality, Scarborough stood under six-feet, weighed about 150 pounds and his hair was brown. He did wear a moustache.

Attorney J.F. Cunningham, who spent fifty years in Texas courts, praised men like Scarborough as among the best of their time, "as game as any men I ever knew." Scarborough spent plenty of time in court defending himself against murder charges for carrying out his duties as a lawman.

On June 29, 1895, he and two fellow officers were involved in the killing of Texas cattle rustler Martin Morose. As before, he won acquittal. The following April, he got involved in another killing, this time in El Paso, Texas. His victim was John Selman, the gunman who had shot John Wesley Hardin in the back of the head while Hardin stood at the bar of a saloon. For the third time, Scarborough stood trial for murder. Although acquitted, he was forced to resign as Deputy US Marshal.

On April 5, 1900, Scarborough was wounded in a gun battle with cattle rustlers in San Simon, Arizona. He was transported to his home in Deming and had his leg amputated. The following day, George Scarborough died. He was 41.

FORTY-NINE

HE COULD OUTSTARE A MAD COBRA

SETH BULLOCK SPENT MUCH OF THE DAY ARRANGING DISPLAYS OF MERCHANDISE AT HIS NEW HARDWARE STORE WHEN HE HEARD GUNFIRE ECHO THROUGH THE STREETS OF DEADWOOD, SOUTH DAKOTA.

The shooting, he learned, came from Nuttal & Mann's saloon on Main Street. Jack McCall had gunned down Wild Bill Hickok with a bullet to the back of the head while he sat playing poker. An impromptu camp-court later found McCall not guilty. After he was released, McCall left town. The verdict eventually triggered a demand among citizens for tougher law enforcement is the crime-ridden community. Since Deadwood was located on Indian land, a governmental entity didn't exist.

Before getting in the hardware business, Seth Bullock served as a legislator and a lawman. Born in Canada, July 24, 1847, he made his way into the United States and, twenty years later, settled in Helena, Montana. A few years later, he ran for the Territorial Senate, and won, and served the two-year term, 1871-1872. During his time as a legislator, he helped create *Yellowstone National Park*.

Bullock stayed busy for the next two years and then ran for election as sheriff of Lewis and Clark County, Montana, and won. Bullock and partner Sol Star decided to open a hardware store. They experienced so much success they decided to expand and headed for Deadwood.

After Hickok's murder, Governor John L. Pennington of Dakota Territory appointed Bullock as Lawrence County sheriff because of his previous experience as a law officer. Bullock wasted no time in flexing his muscles of authority as sheriff, and his presence commanded instant respect. Tall, with gray eyes, bushy eyebrows, and a sweeping thick mustache, Bullock's grandson once remarked, "He could outstare a mad cobra or a rogue elephant." Wasting no time, Bullock appointed a crew of tough and capable deputies to settle disputes over mining claims, and track down outlaws and road agents. He even organized a militia to defend against Indian attacks. All the while, he, and Star operated their store amidst the violence seeping through Deadwood.

In 1884, he was named a deputy US Marshal in western Dakota Territory. In the same year, he met and became close friends with Theodore Roosevelt who, at the time, had been serving as deputy sheriff of Medora, North Dakota. Bullock was also a member of Roosevelt's Rough Riders. The president later appointed the lawman as the first Forest Supervisor for the Black Hills.

FIFTY

SMALL TOWN LAWMEN

T HE MEN WHO WORE THE BADGES IN COMMUNITIES OF THE
AMERICAN WEST HAD TO BE DILIGENT WHEN IT CAME TO
ENFORCING THE LAW. SMALL TOWN SHERIFFS OFTEN WORKED
ALONE. THE MORE FORTUNATE WERE ABLE TO HIRE A PART-TIME
DEPUTY OR TWO FOR MINIMAL WAGES.

Communication about various crimes and criminals was almost
non-existent, except for the telegraph, but only in certain areas.
Descriptions of criminals, their names, and last known locations
were often delivered through the US mail, word-of-mouth, or via
crude drawings on wanted posters—if a printing press were available. These posters got the most visibility when nailed to the walls
of post offices, where everyone went get their mail.

Information traveled at a snail's pace in those days. By the time
notices of criminal activity reached a particular law official, they

were outdated and unreliable. The most-effective kind of sheriff took a proactive role in the enforcement of frontier justice. For example, the first thing a good lawman was monitored the arrival of strangers in their towns—who they were, where they were staying, and why they were visiting.

For the most part, some Western communities took their time establishing a law-enforcement arm. Many of settlers who founded the towns often were immigrants who fled their home country where they had encountered police abuse and harassment. They harbored a natural distrust for the law. As a result, these citizens became the enforcers and formed vigilante committees they kept under their tight control.

There were instances, of course, where the town's sheriffs just happened to be criminals themselves. Some changed, went straight, and did their best to uphold the law. Others used their position for financial and political gain, and influence. Wearing a badge happened to be good cover. It was rare for someone to challenge how they were handling the job, or risk accusing them of wrongdoing. In the case of murders or cattle rustling, small-town lawmen were almost powerless because there was little they could do alone. These kinds of crime were too widespread to be dealt with by just one man.

Because the law was spread so thin, it marked the perfect opportunity for the advent of bounty hunters, men who were strictly in the hunt for reward money. Entrepreneurs also recognized that a gap existed in law enforcement and acted to create private companies to provide services, the most famous of which was Pinkerton National Detective Agency.

The sheriff was usually an elected county official. Some towns, however, appointed marshals and constables, which gave the town's political hierarchy more control over law enforcement. A US marshal, on the other hand, was a federal appointee, responsible for pursuing criminals who broke federal laws. A number of communities hired both a county sheriff and a town marshal, which sometimes created intense animosity and rivalry.

Little glamour was associated with role of sheriff, unlike what has been portrayed on the silver screen. In reality, they spent much of their time serving subpoenas and issuing summons. Lawmen were also responsible for seizing property as directed by civil rulings. And, they often had to issue summons for a coroner's jury. Much of their daily work was mundane. As lawmen became more visible, daily life improved for the better. Citizens began to recognize the authority and need for a legitimate, organized enforcement process, which gave way to a more peaceful way of life.

FIFTY-ONE

BADGE, GUN
& PEN

O N THE NIGHT OF NOV. 23, 1868, EDWARD FRANKLIN, ONE OF
THE TWO MEN WHO HEADED THE MUSGROVE-FRANKLIN GANG,
FELL ASLEEP IN HIS BED AT THE OVERLAND HOUSE IN GOLDEN,
COLORADO.

A lawman, carrying a lighted candle, guided David Cook of
the Rocky Mountain Detective Agency and several other officers
along the darkened hotel hallway, where they managed to slip into
Franklin's hotel room without being detected. Authorities had
already apprehended L.H. Musgrove, the other gang leader, and
put him behind bars in Denver. The gang had terrorized northern
Colorado and southern Wyoming, stealing livestock and committing robbery and murders.

Franklin, and Sanford Duggan, an escaped killer and member of the gang, had devised a plan to free Musgrove, but Cook

got wind of it and discovered where Franklin was hiding. When Franklin, who had been sleeping, rolled over, he saw the flickering candlelight and sat up.

"Franklin, we want you," said Cook, his voice quiet and determined.

"The hell you do."

"Yes, come quietly," Cook added, approaching Franklin with handcuffs.

Franklin grabbed at the loaded revolver he kept under his pillow, but one of the officers struck him with his gun and he fell to the other side of the bed. He then leaped to his feet and, according to a report in the *Denver Post*, pounded his chest in defiance, vowing to die first, "but I'll die hard." With those words, he lunged for a revolver on a nearby table. Guns flashed in the darkened room, Cook and officer Frank Smith firing at the same time. The two bullets struck Franklin in the heart less than an inch apart.

When Denver citizens heard about the incident the following day, a mob gathered and stormed the Larimer Street prison, dragged Musgrove from his cell, and lynched him. Duggan was captured in Cheyenne on December 2nd, and taken back to Denver where vigilantes waited with a hangman's noose.

A dance hall stands at the site of the original hotel. Every now and then, peculiar noises can be heard from the area where Edward Franklin was shot and killed, apparently making true on his promise to "die hard," even though the Overland was destroyed over a hundred years ago.

⁓∽⊛∾⁓

David Cook brought more than 3,000 outlaws to justice and built his reputation on getting results. He served as a counterespionage agent for the Union Army during the Civil War, tracking down Confederate spies, and investigating various crimes, including gold smuggling. The experience made him a natural for law enforcement work and, after the war, he opened the Rocky Mountain Detective Association, based in Denver, a group of law enforcement officers, which operated throughout the region for 35 years.

During the 1870s, Cook served as city marshal of Denver, Arapahoe County Sheriff, and general of the Colorado militia. Considered fearless, Cook was an expert horseman and a crack shot with both rile and handgun. Cook, however, had a bit of literary talent, as well, and decided his experiences as a lawman could help others who never held such a post. No formal training or standards existed for positions in law enforcement in the developing west. Anyone who got the job of sheriff or marshal pretty much made up things as they went along.

In 1882, Cook published a memoir, *Hands Up! or Twenty Years of Detective Work in the Mountains and on the Plains*. Rumors existed that he had the help of a ghostwriter. In the book, he created a set of basic rules called *Self Preservation*. Cook never struck anyone without a reason, according to various historical accounts. At the same time, he never hesitated to kill when the situation demanded.

FIFTY-TWO

SMALL, SIMPLE, & SECRET

THE MAN IN THE CUTAWAY COAT LEANED BACK IN THE CHAIR, GLANCED DOWN AT HIS CARDS, AND DECIDED TO PUSH THE BET HIGHER. ALTHOUGH GUNS WERE OUTLAWED IN TOWN, HE KNEW SUCH AN ORDINANCE COULDN'T PREVENT TROUBLE FROM A SORE LOSER. THANKS TO AN EASTERNER, THE FRONTIER GAMBLER CARRIED A SMALL POCKET PISTOL IN HIS VEST.

Henry Deringer became consumed with making a perfect single-shot pistol, the kind that could be easily concealed and carried in a pocket. The idea of surprise in self-defense situations intrigued him. Deringer foresaw a distinct advantage of being able to carry a palm-sized firearm for this purpose, as long it was accurate at short range.

Deringer, born 1786 in Easton, Pennsylvania, grew up the son Henry Deringer Sr., a colonial gunsmith who made Kentucky rifles. After serving an apprenticeship in his father's shop, and for a gunsmith in Virginia, the younger Deringer decided to set up his own business in 1806 in Philadelphia. Over the years, Deringer earned a reputation for producing quality rifles, muskets, and pistols.

Between 1852 and 1868, he produced the *Philadelphia Deringer.* Competitors across the country understood the marketability of such a weapon and began producing their own, calling it the *Derringer,* using two "*r*" s. Manufacturers copied the design in every detail except, of course, for the misspelled name. In fact, the misspelling soon became an alternate generic term for any pocket-pistol, or *palm* pistol. Deringer underestimated the popularity of his design and never patented it.

These kinds of pistols were originally designed specifically for women. They were called *muff pistols* because women carried them in a muff—those thick, furry tubular cases used to keep their hands warm, and sometimes doubled as a handbag. At one point, negative publicity surfaced about Deringers. The pistol was reputed to be a favorite tool of assassins. The most infamous case centered on John Wilkes Booth who used a Deringer to kill President Abraham Lincoln.

The Deringer also became known as the gambler's gun. Many gamblers - especially lady gamblers - kept a palm pistol in a place where it could easily be accessed. Before long, outlaws saw the value of a pocket pistol because of the element of surprise it provided. The Derringer was also called the *belly gun* because its short barrel made it convenient to use in close quarters.

In towns where ordinances were in force restricting the carrying of firearms, such as Dodge City, many cowboys kept a derringer hidden in a vest pocket or his boot. The single-shot guns were only useful in up-close situations. Accuracy and range suffered dramatically at more than a few feet.

The original Philadelphia Deringer was usually sold in pairs for about $25. They were often used as back-up weapons. According to Bat Masterson, Wild Bill Hickok carried a pair of derringers. Another account revealed that an Arizona lawman carried as many as a half-dozen derringers on him.

FIFTY-THREE

A SPY'S
LAST SUNRISE

O N THE MORNING OF SEPTEMBER 25, 1863, THE PRISONER
STOOD AT THE WINDOW OF HIS CELL IN RICHMOND, VIRGINIA,
AND GAZED AT THE SUNRISE IN THE DISTANT HORIZON. HE
CONSIDERED THIS PARTICULAR SUNRISE THE MOST IMPORTANT OF
HIS YOUNG LIFE. IT WOULD BE HIS LAST.

Situated in one of the three redbrick tobacco warehouses that
made up Castle Thunder prison, Spencer Kellogg Brown spent
about a year confined to the building that housed political prisoners and suspected Union spies. Less than a week before, Brown
went on trial for spying on the Confederacy, and found guilty, and
sentenced to hang. In the days leading up to the trial, Brown sent
his sister, Kitty, a letter acknowledging his hopeless situation. With
a courage far surpassing his age, Brown wrote, "But don't mourn,
Kitty, as for one without hope. These only take away the mortal life,
but God, I trust, has given me one that is immortal."

The Kansas-born Brown grew up a passionate abolitionist, having witnessed his family home burned to the ground in the sack of Osawatomie by pro-slavery forces. On August 30, 1856, he was captured and taken to Lafayette County, Missouri, where he lived in a pro-slavery house in an effort to adjust his thinking. Five years later, he joined the Union Army, using the name Spencer Kellogg to avoid suspicion, having been told the name "Brown" wasn't a safe one to have in Kansas.

He eventually enlisted in the Navy and served on the Essex, a Union ship on the Mississippi River. The Essex played a key role in destroying the Confederate Navy along the Mississippi, including the Confederate Ironclad, Arkansas. When Brown learned the military needed intelligence about troop strengths and shore batteries, he volunteered to collect what information he could. He and someone named Trussel ended up aboard the Confederate ship Charm pretending to be Union deserters. Brown even handcuffed his own hands to sell the story.

After several weeks observing positions of armament and other intelligence, he convinced the commanding officer to allow him to go ashore so he could join the Confederate army. He eventually got away to meet with General U.S. Grant and provided him his findings about enemy positions and the location of various fortifications. Brown then rejoined those on the Essex. When he learned of the Union Navy's concern about a ferry boat resupplying Fort Hudson in Georgia, he volunteered to lead a mission to destroy the ferry boat before the navy launched an attack against the fort. Brown assembled a group of men and sunk the ferry and all its supplies.

On August 15, 1862, young Spencer Kellogg Brown's luck ran out. He was arrested as a spy and imprisoned at Castle Thunder. A year later, on a Friday afternoon, a group of Confederate soldiers took Brown from his cell and escorted him to the gallows at Camp Lee where a large crowd had gathered. The head of the prison,

Captain Alexander, read the charges aloud, ending with the words, "hanged by the neck until dead."

The following day, a brief notice published in the Richmond *Sentinel* summed up Spencer Kellogg Brown's life in one sentence: "This person, convicted of desertion and of being a spy, was hanged yesterday at Camp Lee, in the presence of the military and a large concourse of citizens." He was the third spy to be hanged in Richmond.

One historical irony involved the Brown name. In 1859, the Union hanged radical abolitionist John Brown for treason. The Confederacy hanged Spencer Kellogg Brown for spying but he lived his life as an avid abolitionist. The two weren't related but were neighbors.

Spencer Kellogg Brown was 21 years old.

ABOUT THE AUTHOR

Tom Rizzo is a storyteller, blogger, and speaker. He writes novels, short stories, and nonfiction. His post-Civil War action-adventure novel, *Last Stand At Bitter Creek* ranked among the finalists for the 2013 Western Fictioneers' *Peacemaker Award* for Best First Novel.

A former journalist, Tom worked as a news broadcaster, spent several years with the Associated Press, and worked as a freelance writer creating everything from magazine articles to advertising and promotional material for a broad range of businesses. During his writing journey, he met a colorful cast of characters who inspired him to consider telling stories of his own.

Tom grew up in Central Ohio, lived in Great Britain for several years, and now calls Houston, Texas, home. He is a member of *Western Writers of America, Wild West History Association*, and *Western Fictioneers.*

Learn more about Tom at *www.TomRizzo.com* where he writes blogs about Frontier America. He also interviews veteran and emerging storytellers from various genres. Connect with him:

- Email: *tom@tomrizzo.com*
- Facebook: *https://www.facebook.com/thomas.rizzo.writes*
- Twitter: *https://twitter.com/TomRizzoWrites*
- Amazon: *http://bit.ly/RizzoAmazon*

www.ingramcontent.com/pod-product-compliance
Lightning Source LLC
Chambersburg PA
CBHW060242050426
42448CB00009B/1556